CO CYPRUS
the island of aphrodite

Including Recipes of Taverna Meze

BY
NEARCHOS NICOLAOU
(NICOLAS)

FIRST EDITION 1979
SECOND EDITION 1980
THIRD EDITION 1981
FOURTH EDITION 1982
FIFTH EDITION 1983
REPRINTED 1984
SIXTH EDITION 1985
SEVENTH EDITION 1986
EIGHTH EDITION 1987
REPRINTED 1989

THE BEST SELLER OF ITS KIND PRICE CY£3.00

9th Edition March 1989
First Published March 1979

Copyright 1979 NEARCHOS NICOLAOU
Member of U.C.T.W.J. (Union of Cypriot Tourist Writers and Jurnalist) and F.I.J.E.T. (International)
P.O.Box 4153 NICOSIA—CYPRUS

I.S.B.N. 9963-7516-0-1

OTHER PUBLICATIONS BY N. NICOLAOU

■ TREASURES FROM CYPRUS Coloured Souvenir Book ISBN 9963-7516-6-0
■ GERICHTE AUS ZYPERN German Edition ISBN 9963-7516-4-4
■ CUISINE DE CHYPRE French Edition ISBN 9963-7516-2-3
■ MATLAGNING FRAN CYPERN Swedish Edition ISBN 9963-7516-I-X
■ AL TAHOU MEN COBROS Arabian Edition ISBN 9963-7516-3-6
■ ΜΑΓΕΙΡΙΚΗ ΑΠΟ ΤΗΝ ΚΥΠΡΟ Greek Edition ISBN 9963-7516-7-9
■ ΚΥΠΡΙΑΚΗ ΚΑΙ ΔΙΕΘΝΗΣ ΜΑΓΕΙΡΙΚΗ Greek Edition ISBN 9963-7516-5-2

Cover : P.A.P. GRAPHICS LTD
Phototype: PHOTOGRAMMA LTD
Printed: S.O.G.E.K. LTD
General Distributors: VRAKAS PUBLISHING TEL. 02-462924 CYPRUS

CONTENTS

Page

PRESENT TO THE AUTHOR

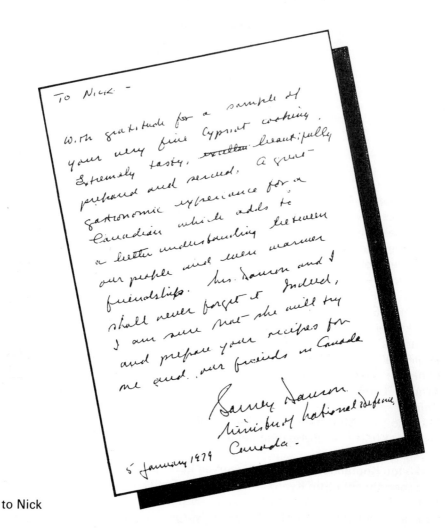

to Nick

With gratitude for a sample of your fine Cypriot cooking. Extremely tasty, beautifully prepared and served. A great gastronomic experience for a Canadian which adds to a better understanding between our people and even warmer friendship. Mrs Dansen and I shall never forget it and indeed I am sure that she will try and prepare your recipes for me and our friends in Canada.

S. Dansen
Minister of National Defence
Canada.

5 January 1979

PRESENT TO THE AUTHOR

The Minister of National Defence of Canada, His Excellency J. Dansen, gives the author a present in appreciation of the Cyprus food which he prepared for him during his visit to Cyprus in January 1979.

TO NICK
WITH THANKS FOR A MAGNIFICENT
DINNER

Minister of National Defence

6 JAN 79

Canada

DEDICATION

This book is dedicated to my beloved wife Eleni for her invaluable contribution to its edition and especially for her help in giving me the exact proportions of the recipes which are included. Since she was very young (like all Cypriot girls then), she started learning from her mother, the secrets of Cypriot food. She has now become, I dare say, one of the best cooks in Cyprus.

With gratitude,
the author.

GREETINGS

It is with great pleasure that I greet the 9th edition of the valuable book of Mr Nearchos Nicolaou and the fact that this book is in its 9th edition in English, is a proof of success as a gastronomical guide for our English speaking, visitors.

This book is a complete guide which has filled up a gap in our services which we offer to tourists like the year-long sunshine, the sea, the history and tradition of this country. Since ancient times the Cyprus cousine is well-known and it was natural that this island gifted by nature to produce fresh vegetables, fruits and distinguished wines whice were even preferred by king Solomon. Through the years the Cyprus cuisine was enriched by the various people who came in Cyprus either as conquerors or as visitors and as a result the Cyprus cuisine has become famous well-wide.

I thank and congratulate Mr Nearchos Nikolaou for his invaluable contribution for maintaining and promoting the tradition of the Cyprus cuisine and I wish to all readers Cypriots and visitors, "Bon Appetite". Quoting the Ex Minister and Chairman of Cyprus Tourism Organisation, Mr. Frixos Petrides said, "here, food is ambrosia and wine is nectar".

A. ANDRONICOU
Director General
Cyprus Tourism Organisation

GREETINGS

It is with pleasure that I hail the issue of the book "Cooking from Cyprus" by Mr Nearchos Nicolaou. Mr Nearchos Nicolaou was one of my students when in 1963 I was responsible for the courses organised for the training of waiters and cooks for hotels and entertainment places. It is worth mentioning that Mr Nearchos Nicolaou was awarded the first prize after winning highest mark in the exams.

I believe that "Cooking from Cypurs" closes a gap with the wealth of recipes (dishes, pastries, drinks) which he introduces.

The recipes are simply written so that the reader can easily follow and execute them.

I conclude with my congratulations and a wish that many Cypriots and foreigners will try the "tasteful recipes" of Mr Nicolaou in order to give him the satisfaction that he has contributed to our country's art of gastronomy.

ELENI PROTOPAPA
Supervisor, Home Economics

GREETINGS

It is with great pleasure that I hail this praiseworthy initiative of Mr Nearchos Nicolaou, because this work is in line with my own thoughts and efforts for the presentation and development of traditional cookery in Cyprus.

This issue is a careful presentation aiming at the continuation of the island's traditional cookery, enriched with the dishes which have been lately introduced or developed through past experiences.

Our author, experienced master of catering arts, introduces us to a rich selection of substances prepared out of the art of cookery, as he himself has lived it and learned it, both at work and at his home, as well as at the homes of his grandma, his mother, his wife, his relatives and friends.

But the author goes beyond the traditional art of cookery. He steps us to contemporary cookery and also undertakes the very recent influences he got from western countries, which indeed have greatly influenced the nutrition of Cypriots, especially the youth.

Unfortunately, we go through a period in which we adopt our nutritional habits with the habits and kitchens of other countries which had, centuries before, based their art on Greek cookery.

But nonetheless, our author, rightly deems this adaptation necessary, since he refers to current human needs, and offers an outlet to the traditional problem of our time. However the purpose of this fine issue is not to research of study the sciense of the art of cookery during the past years.

I congratulate warmly Mr Nearchos Nicolaou for this useful work and I wish him to keep up his good work and try to improve nutrition in Cyprus.

P.V. KONTOPYRGOS MHCIMA
Director of the Hotel and Catering
Institute (H.C.I.)

GREETINGS

Gastronomy, through its cultural expression has made a special course in Greek history.

The symposiums of ancient Greeks, which were held in a climate of fertility with the great and important things of human life then taking place, have left their mark and influenced contemporary gastronomy.

Apart from the biological necessity, the taste and the preservation of customs and traditions, gastronomy has gained an important place in the field of education, bibliography and technology.

Cyprus was lucky enough to have, in our times, valuable continuators of gastronomic tradition.

The author of this book deserves a special place among them. His profundity knowledge and unique technique established him as a MASTER of Cypriot gastronomy and international cookery.

In his new book of dishes, which he arranged in such a digestible way for the reader, while the instructions of their preparation are simple and applicable even to the most ... unskilful in cookery.

The detailed description of ingredients, time and quantity in a practical way make his volume of Mr Nearchos Nicolaou a model MANUAL of Cyprus cookery.

Cyprus meze, legumes, soupes, pastes, meats and fish food, the salads, the pastries and drinks are introduced in the book in matching combinations, whose preparation along with the garnish have upgrated cookery into a real art.

My association through a special friendship with Nearchos Nicolaou, which is kept alive through the Union of Cypriot Journalists and Travel Writers, has given me the opportunity to meet this fine man and set familiar with his work, which honours him and our country. It benefits Cyprus and places it high in the field of International Gastronomy.

GEORGE NICOLAOU
President of the Union of
Cypriot Journalists and Travel Writers
Member of the executive Committee of the
World Federation F.I.J.E.T.

PREFACE

I have spent most of my life involved in the arts of cooking and of running restaurants. I have loved this profession since I was very young and especially when I started getting well into its science. Almost forty years have passed since then, and the more I study this science, the more I realise I still have much to learn.

My profession gives me the opportunity to come into contact with and talk to a lot of foreigners, such as tourists and businessmen. All of them have always assured me of their great love of Cypriot food, and of their enjoyment of being in Cyprus itself. I know that this is not said just to flatter us, nor to give meaningless compliments, not even to show good manners. Thousands of tourists who visit us every year come up with the same confession: "This island gives us a lot of riches. The natural beauties, the open-hearted and hospitable people, and the delicious food which literally enslaves us!"

Their nice words and admiration made me feel really happy and proud. However, I was not pleased with my simple answer: "Thank you", so I thought that I should offer something to these people; a reply to everything I hear every day from them. I should also do something for my own country which offers so lavishly everything it has to each visitor. I took the decision; to write this informative and simple book for the people who love Cyprus and its food, for those who want to "carry" with them the food which they have tasted here, for the emigrants and finally for anybody who wants to try Cypriot food. I believe I am doing my duty here in Cyprus, for its friends and for all those who would like to meet us.

Thank you,
the author.

Our wealth... is our people, they will tell you all the secrets about Cyprus

 CYPRUS TOURISM ORGANISATION

FOR TOURIST INFORMATION PLEASE APPLY TO—

CYPRUS TOURISM ORGANISATION
18, Th. Theodotou Street,   Tel. (02) 443374
Telex 2165, P.O.B. 4535, Nicosia or

1. TOURIST INFORMATION BUREAUX IN CYPRUS

NICOSIA
LAIKI YITONIA   Tel. (02) 444264

LIMASSOL
15, SPYROU ARAOUZOU STR.,   Tel. (051) 62756

LARNACA
DEMOCRATIAS SQUARE   Tel. (041) 54322
LARNACA INTERNATIONAL AIRPORT   Tel. (041) 54389

PAPHOS
3. GLADSTONE STREET   Tel. (061) 32841
PAPHOS AIRPORT   (061) 36833
AYIA NAPA   Tel. (037) 21796
PLATRES   Tel. (054) 21316

2. TOURIST OFFICES ABROAD:

UNITED KINGDOM
CYPRUS TOURIST OFFICE
213. REGENT STREET LONDON W1, R8 DA,
Tel. 01-734 9822 Telex: LDN 22540 CYTOUR

F.R. of GERMANY
FREMDENVERKEHRSZENTRALE ZYPERN
6 FRANKFURT am MAIN 1 KAISERSTRASSE 13
Tel. (0611) 284708 Telex: 414137 CTO FRD

SWITZERLAND
FREMDENVERKEHRSZENTRALE ZYPERN
Gottfried - Keller - Strasse 7
8001 ZURICH
Tel. (01) 693303 Telex: 815100 CTOZ

FRANCE
OFFICE DU TOURISM DE CHYPRE
15, Rue de lu Paix, 75002 PARIS
Tel. (1) 2614249 Telex: 610664 PARIS

SWEDEN
CYPRIOTISKA STATENS TURISTBUR()
VASAGATAN 11 S 111 - 35 STOCKHOLM
Tel. 08/115578 Telex: 15718

GREECE
CYRPUS TOURISM ORGANISATION
36. Voukourestiou street, ATHENS GREECE
Tel. 3610178 Telex: 214120 ATHENS

ITALY
ENTE NAZIONALE PER IL TOURISMO DI CIPRO
6. Via S. Sofia, 20122 Milano
Tel. 02-866617. Telex 320058

UNITED STATES
CYPRUS TRADE CENTRE
13. EAST 40TH STR., NEW YORK 10016,
TEL. (212) 688-6016

BAHRAIN
CYRPUS TOURIST OFFICE
P.O.Box 45, MANAMA, BAHRAIN
Tel. 243592/3, Telex 7038 CYTOUR BN

COOK'S NOTE

'CUP'

A Cypriot cook's cup is only a convenient approximation. Usually a tea cup is used (about 12 ounces imperial). This should be considered for all of the following recipes.

SALT AND PEPPER

In most of my recipes when referring to salt and pepper, I say nothing about their quantity. The reason is that I don't know every reader's taste. In Cyprus there is a saying: "Pará na tróis tze na ftínnis kálio na tróis tze na rtínnis". Its meaning is this: It is better to put salt and pepper when you start eating, rather than add the salt and pepper beforehand, and then not to be able to eat the food, because it is too salty.

"SKORDHO" — GARLIC*

Garlic has become a very popular topic in our time. Recently in many Medical Congresses in European countries, such announcements as "garlic against cancer", "garlic against tuberculosis" "garlic cures asthma", "garlic is good for sex" were made. In our opinion man for thousands of years used garlic as a wonderful and miraculous spice. Let us see, in short, the history of this small bulb that was and still is used so much by mankind.

Garlic was known and cultivated by man 5,000 years ago. For many years it was used as a medicine, and was thought to be irreplaceable. It was used against colds, against venereal diseases and it was supposed to be the magic plant of love. The great gastronome — Maitre Margo Oliver whom I greatly admire and respect, says in a note: In Weekend Magazine, Jan. 28, 1978: "The Roman historians and connoisseurs Pliny and Elder insist that 61 illnesses can be cured by garlic". Pharmacists of the Middle-Ages, believed in its great pharmaceutical qualities and considered it to have better results than any other plants or herbs. So they recommended it without any restraint as a cure to many illnesses like high blood pressure, toothache, lack of appetite, freckles, for insect or snakebites, whooping cough, cough, baldness, shivering, various diseases of the nervous system, general weakening, tapeworm, and others. They used to eat it (like we do today) or take it with some water like a pill, smell it or crush it and put it in their ears, their teeth, their abdomen and elsewhere. The parents, also, crushed it lightly, and put the pulp in their children's feet, believing that garlic oil would cure them. The doctors of those ancient times, before they visited a sick person, made sure that they had lots of cloves of garlic with them. Eastern scientists believed that garlic was wonderful not only for the skin, but that it could also help improve their mental capabilities. Ancient Egyptians piously respected it and took oaths in its name, believing it was God's gift to man. The ancient Greek historian Herodotus describing the building of the famous Giza pyramid says: "The 10,000 people, who, for 20 whole years were working, transferring the 2,300,000 large stones in the place where the pyramid was to be built, used to live in food mainly made of garlic and onions." The Roman nobles used to give garlic to their slaves for more energy and their soldiers for greater courage and bravery. In India, people always carry garlic with them as "magic amulet" so that it may protect them from "evil eye" and "malice".

In Cyprus we notice that many mothers hide garlic in their babies' clothes to keep, as they say, malice away. Finally, today we see that this "magic" plant after all these thousands of years is still helpfull to mankind. What shocks us is the garlic's smell when it is fresh. It is no secret that the best specialities which are preferred by people, contain a portion of fresh garlic.

In Cypriot cooking garlic is lavishly used in almost every dish. They use it for its many good qualities. Be careful though, not to overcook it because it will lose its flavour.

Note: Each recipe that contains garlic will be marked by an asterisk (*) for easy reference.

"MEZEDHES"
CYPRUS HORS - D' OEUVRES

It is almost essential for every Cypriot who drinks wine or any other alcoholic drink, to have something to eat at the same time. The "something" that accompanies his drink is called "meze" and it can be just a handful of salty broad beans or a piece of smoked kippers or any other dish, as long as they are all served in small quantities and chopped in small pieces.

This custom began hundreds of years ago, when the majority of men were farmers or cattlemen, and they only drank on special occasions. Such occasions were usually feasts "xefandomata" celebrating religious days, birthdays, weddings, or deaths. Of course, once the men were given an excuse, they were not content to drink in moderation; one had to drink a considerable amount of alcohol to really "feast". "Feasting" "xephandoma" for them was an endless "service" which lasted for many hours, perhaps even a whole day. They took their time eating and drinking; they sang (and everybody had to participate in those never-ending songs), they told jokes and they "philosophised" about life. The continuous offering of new kinds of delicacies, or "mezedhes", which stimulated their appetites and encouraged more drinking, was another reason for such prolonged "feasting".

These delicacies, which were produced unceasingly by the housewife and her children, were always served in small quantities, and cut in small pieces. During such "gatherings" or "feasts", the hosts ought to present their guests with their very best food and drink, which they saved with care for these special occasions.

Wine always flowed in copious quantities. Usually it was "zivania", a kind of liquor which is produced by the distillation of grapes, in most cases by the host himself.

1

Pork was a common meat for the cypriots, and out of the various parts of the pig, they skillfully made their most delicious "mezedhes". Usually, they slaughtered the pigs during Christmas time. All Cypriots, even the poorest had to have their own pigs. For example, the famous smoked ham, which we still have today, was made out of the back leg of the pig which was smoked over the fireplace. The front legs of the pig were cut into small pieces, and the intestines were made into delicious Cypriot smoked sausages. The ribs of the animal were salted well, smoked and used as "bacon", all through the year.

The famous "zalatina" was made out of the head, together with the trotters. Finally, the remaining parts were cut into big pieces, fried, put into pots made out of clay and were covered with the boiled fat of the animal.

With the pork specialities, the Cypriots served other dishes, such as the "apokti", a salted piece of meat, usually kid, which was cooked by simply leaving it in the sun.

With the wild herbs gathered in the fields and fresh vegetables from the garden, the Cypriots made pickles called "ksidhata". They also pickled various birds and rabbits in vinegar.

During the harvest season, people dried fruit in the sun, and kept them for "mezedhes". During the grape harvest they made raisins, "soutzioukko" and "palouzé" from almonds and grape juice. In addition they gathered wild mushrooms and snails as well as crabs and eels, which were then abundant in the rivers of Cyprus. They also offered as "mezedhes" dairy products, domestic birds, rabbits and so on.

The people, in those days, did not give much importance to their everyday diet. What was significant for them, was not only to have everything that was needed for the "feasting", "xephandoma", but also, to have everything in vast amounts, so as not to feel embarassed in case of lack of food.

In these early feasts we find the most probable origin "meze", a tradition which has been passed from generation to generation. To test this theory, ask somebody "what is a 'meze'?" He will answer briefly: "Different kinds of food, hot or cold, which are served at certain intervals and always in small quantities, so as to keep them fresh and hot". The modern "meze" has lost some of the character and grandeur of the feasts of yesterday. The modern taverns and the expensive restaurants have now taken over. Nevertheless, the various kinds of "mezedhes" are still very popular among tourists and Cypriots alike.

We shall try to present to you below, most of these "mezedhes": the most famous and most popular ones.

"MEZEDHES KRIYI" — COLD MEZEDHES

"SCORDHALIA" — GARLIC BREAD SAUCE*

This sauce is used for various salads of boiled vegetables and especially for boiled fillet of fish or fried fish.

6 cloves of garlic
2 cups of bread soaked in water
    and drained
1 cup of olive oil
$^1/_3$ cup of vinegar
½ tsp of salt
Finely chopped parsley
    and 4—5 black olives.

Crush garlic until it becomes like a paste and put it in a bowl. Add salt and bread, a little at a time, stirring at the same time to make a smooth paste. Keep on stirring, adding olive oil and vinegar, drop by drop, until the mixture becomes a thick sauce. Put it in another bowl and garnish with finely chopped parsley and 4—5 black olives.

Makes about 2 pints.

Note: Some people use the same quantity of mashed potatoes instead of bread. Half a cup of walnuts or almonds well crushed can be added to the sauce if desired.

3

"TARAMOSALATA" — FISHROE SAUCE/DIP

Appetizing dip eaten with bread, with all salads, and various boiled vegetables.

> 1 cup of olive oil
> 1 finely chopped onion (small)
> ½ cup of taramas (fishroe)
> 1½ cup of bread soaked and drained
> ½ cup of lemon juice
> ½ tsp of salt
> Chopped parsley, pickled
>   vegetables and black olives,
>   for garnish

If the "taramas" is not ready-made in the box, put it in luke-warm water, for about 30 minutes, to get rid of its salt. Clean and drain well. If however, it is in the box, crush it together with a few drops of olive oil until it becomes a paste. Put paste in a bowl and mix with bread, olive oil and lemon juice, alternately and a little at a time, beat with wire whisk or a mixer until it becomes a thick smooth paste. Garnish with the finely chopped parsley, the pickled vegetables and the black olives, and serve in small bowls.

Make about 2 pints.

Note: If preferred, the bread can be substituted by the same quantity of mashed potatoes.

"TACHINOSALATA" — TACHINI DIP*

This dip is very appetizing when eaten with small pieces of bread or green vegetables.

> 2 cups of tachini (Tachini is made
>   from sesame and it is sold
>   in jars in grocery shops)
> 6 cloves of well crushed garlic
> 1 cup of cold water
> 1 tsp of salt
> 4—5 black olives
> ½ cup of lemon juice
> ½ cup of olive oil
> ½ cup of finely chopped parsley

Put tachini and salt in a bowl and stir together. Add olive oil, lemon juice and water, alternately and a little at a time. Keep stirring until thickening. Stir half of the parsley into the cream.

Serve in small bowl; garnish with the rest of the parsley and 4—5 black olives.

5

"CHIROMERI" — CYPRUS SMOKED HAM

Chiromeri is one of the best Cyprus "mezedhes". It is very popular among Cypriots and famous in other countries too, because of its excellent taste and its delicious aroma. It is served cold, cut in oblong pieces. At the restaurants and hotels it is served as an appetizer accompanied by slices of melon. It can also be served hot, cut in small pieces and fried with eggs as in an omelette.

Its preparation is usually undertaken by villagers in the cold months of winter. This is important because the preparation requires about sixty days.

My father-in-law is 97 years old and he is a specialist in the making of chiromeri. He was taught by his father. This is what he tells us about the complicated way of preparing chiromeri.

Take the skin and the excess fat from the back leg of the pork. Sprinkle with dry red wine and add a thick layer of salt. Put it in a big dish and cover with dry red wine. Press the leg with something heavy so that it is always in the wine. Turn it onto the other side every four days and shake the wine at the same time. It must remain in the wine for about 30 days. After this period of time take it out of the wine and put it over the fireplace so that it becomes smoked. Remove it after two days and put it under big stones or any other kind of heavy weight; leave it like that for two days in order for it to take its thin shape and to reject its water. Then hang it over the fireplace for about 15 days. During this period place it under these heavy weights 3—4 times.

The secret for preserving chiromeri is salt. Use a lot of salt before putting it in the dish. After piercing the bone with a long thick spit, fill it with salt and wine to be absorbed.

When it is ready remove it from the fireplace and keep it in a cool place. It can be preserved for a year or even longer, before it is consumed.

"MELINTZANOSALATA" — EGGPLANT SALAD*

This salad can be served with roast meat and grilled fish or as a "meze".

1 kilo of eggplant
3 cloves of garlic, crushed
½ cup of olive oil
¼ cup of wine vinegar
½ cup of walnuts, chopped (optional)
salt and pepper to taste
Some black olives and some
   finely chopped parsley.

Remove the seeds and the stalk from the eggplant. Put the eggplant in a pan and bake in hot oven for about half an hour. Peel, and place them on a piece of wood. Pound them into pulp with the flat edge of a knife. Put eggplant, garlic, salt and pepper in a bowl alternately, add olive oil and vinegar a little at a time, stirring constantly with a wooden spoon. Add chopped walnuts and keep stirring until the cream becomes smooth. Put it in a big bowl and garnish with the finely chopped parsley and the black olives. Keep the "melintzanosalata" in the refrigerator and serve cold.

Makes about 2 pints.

"KAPARI" — PICKLED CAPER

This is one of the many "mezedhes" which is also used in salad. Caper is a wild bush and twice a year people in Cyprus gather its branches (kapari), its flowers and even its seeds which look like tiny cucumbers; in Spring when its branches are small and tender, and in summer when its flowers are just starting to bloom. The seeds and flowers of caper are pickled in the same way as its fresh branches (Kapari).

After "Kapari" is gathered, it is put into glass or clay jars with enough water to cover it, for about 7—10 days. The water must be changed every day. On the 11th day the "Kapari" is drained and sprinkled with a lot of salt. Then it is dried in the sun and placed in glass jars with enough vinegar to cover it.

"Kapari" may be preserved for a long time. As a "meze" it is served with olive oil and it is quite appetizing. In salads it is cut in smaller pieces and it is mixed with the rest of the vegetables.

7

"KARAOLI VRASTI" — BOILED SNAILS

Snails are abundant in Cyprus and they can be found in the mountains and near dry rivers beds. They are well-loved by the children and they are an appetizing mezé for adults when entertaining. Snail-gathering is extremely pleasant. The young children pray for the rain to stop, in Winter, so that they can go out and gather snails. Groups of people, young and old, are often seen on the mountains gathering this great delicacy. When the gathering is finished, they also gather small bushes of thyme for the special "fasting" that the snails will go through. Firstly a container is filled with wheat chaff. A branch from a thyme bush is placed in the chaff. The snails are put in the container for 3—4 days. This cleans them of all their mucus and other excreta. Now they are ready to be washed and cooked. Snails are cooked in a pot of water with salt and half cup of vinegar. The snails **must** be added to the water when it is still cold. If the water is too warm they will stay in their shells. As the water heats up the snails attempt to escape from the heat, by coming out of their shells. This is important, for otherwise it becomes extremely difficult to shell them. When the snails are cooked, drain and shell them with the help of a tooth pick or a small fork.

After this preparation the snails are put into small bowls and a mixture of beaten olive oil, vinegar, salt and pepper is poured over them to marinate them. They can then be eaten as they are. This cold dish is usually part of the Cypriot mezédhes.

"PSARI SAVORO" — FISH IN SAVOURY SAUCE*

This dish is made with small size fish and is served cold. It is either served as a "meze" or as hors d'oeuvres.

1 kilo of small fish
1 cup of corn oil and
  ½ cup of olive oil
1 cup of wine vinegar
2 cups of cold water
3 cloves of garlic, finely chopped
1 tsp of sugar
1 small spring of rosemary
1½ cup of flour
salt and pepper to taste.

Clean, wash and drain the fish and put them in a bowl. Pour the lemon juice over them and leave them for half an hour. Put salt and pepper in half of the flour and then coat the fish with it. Fry in heated oil and put them in rows in a bowl. Pass the oil, already used, through a fine sieve and put it back into a clean frying-pan. Heat well and put the garlic in the frying-pan until it is golden. Add the rest of the flour, little by little, while stirring at the same time with a wire-whisk. When the paste is brown, add vinegar, sugar, rosemary, and water. Stir until it becomes a soft paste, remove the rosemary and cover the fish with it. Allow to cool and keep in refrigerator until it becomes thicker.

Makes about 4 dishes.

"TALATTOURI" —
SALAD MADE OF YOGHOURT AND CUCUMBER*

One of the Cyprus most famous dishes. It is extremely appetizing and it is served not only as a "meze", but also as a salad accompanying the main dish.

2 cups of yoghourt
3 cloves of garlic, crushed
1 cup of cucumber, cut in very
    thin slices
3 tblsp of olive oil
1 tblsp of vinegar
1 tsp of dried mint
Salt to taste

Put the sliced cucumber on a plate and sprinkle with salt. Let it stand for about half an hour and drain the excess liquid. Put garlic in a bowl and mix it with olive oil and vinegar. Add yoghurt little by little and stir at the same time until it becomes a smooth cream. Drain the cucumber and mix with yoghourt. Put it in the refrigerator. Serve in small plates and sprinkle with a few drops of olive oil and dried mint.

Makes about 4 small dishes.

"DHIAFORI ALLI MEZEDHES" —
VARIOUS OTHER "MEZEDHES"

Raw vegetables, such as artichokes, celery, cabbages, the fresh leaves of lettuce, and others which are served in small pieces with a lot of lemon juice and salt are also considered as "mezedhes".

Cypriot cheese such as "halloumi" and "fetta", are "mezedhes" too.

The various kinds of game, such as fig-eating birds, partridges and wild rabbits are half-cooked in salted water, kept in vinegar and served as "mezedhes".

Tomatoes, cucumbers, celery and various wild plants found in the fields can also be served pickled with olive and salt.

10

"MOUNGRA" — PICKLED CAULIFLOWER

This appetizing Cyprus "meze" is served during periods of fasting or any other time. Its preparation is a bit complicated but it is worth trying.

2 kilos of cauliflower
1 ½ cup of synappi (sinapis — mustard seeds)
1 loaf of unbaked bread about 1 kilo
1 tblsp salt

Five days before the date of its preparation buy an unbaked bread from a bakery and put in a jar so that it becomes yeast. On the sixth day take off the hard leaves of the cauliflower. Cut it in smallish pieces and wash it well. Boil water and salt in a big pan and add some pieces of cauliflower. When the water boils take them out and put some other pieces until all of them are boiled, but not cooked. Pour some cold water over them and drain. Arrange them on clean clothes until they dry. In the meantime crush the "synappi" in a mortar. Make sure all the seeds are well crushed. Also, dissolve the yeast in luke-warm water so that it becomes a thin paste. Put a row of cauliflower in a big clean and well-dried jar. Sprinkle with a little crushed "synappi". Add a second row of cauliflower and sprinkle again with "sinappi". Continue until all the cauliflower is used.

Pour the diluted yeast to cover the cauliflower. Cover the jar with a clean cloth and leave for 8—10 days. Stir twice in 24 hours with a big wooden spoon. On the 10th day "moungra" is ready to be served.

It can be preserved for a month or more, but it must be emphasized that the wooden spoon used for taking some "moungra" out of the jars must be clean. Otherwise it may be spoiled.

"ELIES TSAKISTES" — CRUSHED GREEN OLIVES*

Select some green olives, wash and dry in the sun. Beat them gently with a flat stone or a hammer, in order to split them. Put them in a large jar and add cold water to cover them. The next day the water must be changed and this is repeated for şix consecutive days. Then dissolve salt in water and cover the olives with it. (About, half tsp of salt per cup of water). Add the juice of 3 lemons to the salted water and pour half cup of olive oil on the surface. Store the jar in a cool place. To serve olives, wash them to remove salt and pour olive oil beaten with lemon juice over them. Add, some crushed coriander and some crushed cloves of garlic.

Note: In order to make sure the salted water has got the correct quantity of salt needed, put a fresh egg in it. If it floats, with part of it coming out of the water, then it is just fine.

"OCTAPODHI KSIDHATO" — PICKLED OCTOPUS

Pickled octopus is one of the most well-known and most popular "mezedhes". Select some small, fresh octopus which must be well-beaten so that they are soft and digestible. Wash, and put them in a pan without water; they cook in their own broth which they will discharge. Cook on low heat for about an hour until they soften. Five minutes before they are to be removed from heat, add some salt. Drain in a fine sieve and let them cool. Skin, cut into big pieces and put in a glass jar. Prepare a solution of 1 part water and 3 parts red wine vinegar. Cover the octopus with it. Pour half cup of olive oil on the surface. Store in a cool place. Serve in small pieces, with olive oil beaten with vinegar.

"ZALATINA" — PORK IN LEMON AND VINEGAR JELLY

A delicious Cypriot "meze", especially for the country people for whom it is a favourite. It is prepared from the various parts of the pig's head and its shins. In the towns this food is prepared in different ways, using other kinds of meat, adding pickled vegetables and boiled eggs. For the thickening of the food, commercial gelatine is used; but in my opinion the taste is different and not as good as the countryman's thickened stock, So, I will mention the genuine (original) way of making it. Take a whole or half of a pig's head, according to the quantity wanted. Put in lukewarm water for about half an hour and then wash well with cold water. Put the head in a large pan of cold water with the shins and add some black pepper corns. Boil, and skim the stock occasionally. Then cover the pan and boil head for about two hours or until meat and shins are separated from the bones and the stock reduces to 15—20 cups. Remove the pan from the heat and pass stock through a sieve, into a clean pan. Add wine vinegar to the stock, (3 cups of stock to 1 cup of vinegar) salt and pepper. If preferred, half cup of lemon juice and half cup of bitter oranges juice to 3 cups of stock can be added instead of vinegar. Before all the juice or vinegar is poured into the pan, taste and add as much as needed. Bone all the meat from the head and shins and cut into small pieces as well as tongue and ears and mix together. Put in bowls and cover with stock. Cut red hot peppers into medium pieces and add them to the bowls. Add also small sprig of rosemary. Let the bowls cool and keep in refrigerator.

Note: In order to keep "zalatina" for a long time, use only vinegar.

13

"ZESTI MEZEDHES" — HOT MEZEDHES

"MANITARIA KRASATA" — MUSHROOMS IN WINE

1 kilo of wild mushrooms from the
    mountains, or any other kind
½ cup of butter
½ cup of dry red wine
½ tsp of crushed coriander
Salt and pepper to taste

Wash and boil the mushrooms. Drain and fry in the butter in a small pan until they become light brown. Add the coriander and after 2—3 minutes, the wine. When the contents boil add half cup of water and simmer for about an hour. Remove from pan, add salt and pepper to taste and serve hot.

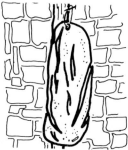

"LOUNTZA" — SMOKED FILET OF PORK

"Lountza" is one of the best Cypriot "mezedhes" and the visitors of the island praise it for its wonderful aroma and interesting taste. It is made of pork loin which is first salted with a lot of salt, then soaked in red dry wine for 8—10 days. Then it is sprinkled with lots of crushed coriander, and hung outside in the sun to dry for 1—2 days. It is then hung by the fire place for 10—15 days to become smoked and dry.

"Lountza" is kept all year round, hung in a cool, dry place. It is served as a "meze" or as an appetizer, cut into thin slices and cooked either on charcoal, or fried with eggs.

14

"PASTOURMAS LOUCANICO" — BEEF AND GARLIC SAUSAGES*

The "pastourmas" is an Armenian speciality. However, because it is well-liked and well-known to all the inhabitants of the island, it is always one of the best "meze". It contains lots of garlic and this makes it very tasty. It may also be served as a first dish before a main meal. In cyprus "pastourmas" is sold in supermarkets or small shops. It is very rare that a housewife will prepare the "pastourma" herself, because the preparation is complicated and it also takes many days to prepare. However, here is the method of preparation, for those who want to know how it is made or for those who want to try and prepare it themselves.

1 bundle of beef intestines
 (1 ½ meter long approx.)
1 kilo of ground beef
1 whole crushed head of garlic
1 tblsp of baked cumin seed, finely
 crushed
1 tblsp of salt
1 tsp of cayenne pepper
½ tsp of pepper

Turn the intestines inside out, wash them in plenty of water and in the last rinse add 1 cup of vinegar. Then hang to drain. Put the meat in a bowl and add the rest of the ingredients. Mix well and leave for half an hour. Fill the intestines with this mixture and fold in two so that it forms two straight parallel lines, one next to the other. Tie the two edges of the folded intestine, tightly, with a piece of string, and then the whole intestine at every 4 inches approximately. With a fork pierce the whole length of the folded intestine. Cover with a thick towel and place a straight thick piece of wooden board over it so that the "pastourmas" is pressed and is gradually drained. Leave for 6—8 hours to drain well and then hang it out in the sun for 4—5 days. Keep it like that in a cool place. Make a slit with a knife and cook over charcoal, or cut in small pieces and fry with scrambled eggs.

Note: The same mixture used for "pastourmas" can also be shaped as a hamburger and cooked on grill.

"KEFTEDHAKIA" — FRIED TINY MEATBALLS

¾ kilo minced pork meat
1 cup of grated potatoes
½ cup of bread crumbs
½ cup of finely chopped parsley
½ cup of finely chopped onion
1 egg
Salt and pepper to taste.

Mix all the ingredients together and knead. Leave for half an hour. Make small meat balls, approximately one tablespoon of minced meat each. Fry in a big pan with hot oil until they get light brown and then place in a platter. They can be served hot or cold.

"HOUMMI KOPANISTI" — CHICK PEA DIP (HOUMMOUS)*

1 cup of tachini
1 cup of lemon juice
3 cups of chick-peas boiled
1 cup of olive oil
½ cup of parsley, finely chopped

5 cloves of crushed garlic
½ tsp of red pepper (vegetable) crushed
1 tblsp of salt

Soak the chick peas in water for about 10 hours over night. Then drain and put in a pan containing clean water and ½ tblsp of salt. Cook for about one hour or until tender.

Put ½ tblsp of salt, red pepper, tachini and garlic in the mixer and beat well for about 5 minutes. Meanwhile, pass the boiled chick peas through a sieve and keep aside half a cup. Add the rest to the tachini mixture and beat well until they become a thick paste. Reduce "speed" and alternately add small quantities of oil and lemon juice.

Finally place the mixture into small bowls and garnish with 5—6 whole chick peas as well as with 4—5 black olives. Sprinkle with finely chopped parsley.

Makes 4—6 dishes.

"SHEFTALIA" —
GRILLED ROLLS OF SPICED MINCED MEAT

"Sheftalia" are very tasty and they are usually served as a hot "meze". In Cyprus, those who decide to drink a glass of wine or two, often include "sheftalia" among their other "mezedhes". "Sheftalia" are cooked on a brazier with charcoal which is usually placed near the table outside in the yard. In this way they can watch the "sheftalia" being cooked and when they are ready they take them out of the spits right into their plates. "Sheftalia" can also be served as a main dish, with "souvlakia" and some fried potatoes. In Cyprus there are shops which sell only "souvlakia" and "sheftalia" mixed and they are put in a kind of bread called "pitta" — bread envolope — together with finely chopped parsley, onion and some pickled vegetables. Their preparation, is very easy; it is worth trying them.

1 kilo of minced meat
  (pork and beef mixed)
1 cup of finely chopped onions
1 cup of finely chopped parsley
1 tsp of dry mint or 2 tsps of
  fresh mint
1 tsp of salt
1 packet of lamb-suet
¼ cup of bread crumbs
½ tsp of cinnamon powder
½ tsp of pepper

Put suet in lukewarm water until it softens. Put all the ingredients in a bowl and knead well. Leave them for about ½ an hour. Cut suet in square pieces 4X4 inches and put onto each piece a tblsp of the prepared mixture. Start rolling, then close the two edges and keep on rolling until there is no more suet. Pierce each "sheftalia" through two spits or a double one, because if we use only one spit "sheftalia" will spin on the spit while cooking. Cook on bright red charcoal. It must be emphasized that the fire must be low, and there should be no flame at all. Turn the spits every 2—3 minutes and cook for 15—20 minutes, until the suet is light brown.

Makes 5—6 dishes.

"KEFTEDHES STA KARVOUNA" — MINCED MEAT ON CHARCOAL

1 kilo of minced veal meat
½ cup of finely chopped onion
½ cup of finely chopped parsley
½ cup of bread-crumbs
½ tblsp dried oregano
salt and pepper to taste

Put all the ingredients except oregano in a bowl, knead them well and leave them for about ½—1 hour. Then, shape the mixture into big round balls and press them slightly to flaten and widen them so that they have a thickness of 1½ cm and a perimeter of 7 cm. While shaping them, dip your hands in cold water so that the shaping becomes easier and at the same time their surface becomes smoother. Spread them with oil and cook them on charcoal for about 5—7 minutes.

I would like to point out that the grill you will use for cooking the meat balls, must be quite hot so that the meat balls do not stick on it.

After they are cooked put them on a platter and sprinkle them with dried oregano powder.

Makes 10—12 pieces.

SOME MORE EGG MEZEDHES

Various mezedhes can be prepared with beaten eggs, as omelettes. We refer to a number of such mezedhes.

Mushrooms with eggs:

These mushrooms are wild and they are picked from the mountains during wintertime. They are big, their shape is like a small plate and their colour is orange. They are cleaned, peeled and cut in small pieces; then they are fried with oil or butter and finally mixed with eggs.

Artichokes with eggs:

Prepared in exactly the same way as mushrooms with eggs.

Wild asparagus with eggs:

This kind of asparagus is gathered from the fields. Their hard part is removed and after they are fried with oil or butter they are mixed with beaten eggs.

18

"PASTOURMAS LOUNTZA" —
VEAL SPICED WITH GARLIC AND CAYENNE PEPPER*

The "Pastourmas Lountza" is the second kind of "pastourmas". The first kind has already been mentioned. The method of preparing it is completely different from the "pastourma loucaniko" because this one is not prepared with minced meat but with a whole meat-piece which is finally hung out in the sun to dry and then cut in thin slices. It is served either cold or fried as it is, or with the addition of beaten eggs. The meat used is veal. It is found in the market and is prepared by specialists in "pastourma" making. The method is supposed to be a secret and is passed on from parents to children or relatives. Here is the "pastourmas lountza" preparation as I heard it myself from these people.

Cut the veal in long thick slices of 10—12 cm thickness. Make long tears in it and fill with salt. Spread salt on the rest of the meat. Wrap in thick cloths and press with a weight for 4—5 days. Then hang out in the sun for another 4—5 days until it is well dried. Prepare a cream with lots of pounded garlic, cayenne pepper, pounded cumin seeds black pepper and salt and cover the meat with it. Hang it again out in the sun for 2 more days and then it is ready. It is an excellent "meze" which is worth trying.

"PATATES ANTINAKTES" —
CRACKED SPRING POTATOES

1 kilo of small spring potatoes
1 cup of corn oil
½ cup of red dry wine
¼ cup of crushed coriander
Salt and pepper to taste

Wash the potatoes well and dry, with a cloth. Hit each one with a mallet to break slightly. Heat the oil well, add the potatoes and fry until they turn reddish-brown, stirring the potatoes frequently by holding the covered pan and shaking well. When potatoes become brown, remove most of the oil. Heat and add the wine, salt, pepper and coriander. Reduce heat and simmer gently with lid on, for another 15—20 minutes. Serve hot. The name of this recipe is taken from the Cypriot word "antinasso" which means toss.

19

"KOUPES" — SPICED MINCED MEAT ENCLOSED IN GROUND WHEAT PASTE

"Koupes" are a kind of appetizer or "meze", very tasty and greatly consumed by the people of Cyprus. They are made out of a ground wheat paste formed into tubular shapes and stuffed with minced meat and spices.

Basically, there are two kinds of "Koupes". The one kind, are the big tubular shaped "Koupes" stuffed with different spices, a lot of onion and minced meat. This kind is sold by wandering sellers in open markets, fairs, and small coffee places.

The second kind of "Koupes", are the small ones that are the size and shape of an egg, and are stuffed with less onion, minced meat, different spices, and pine nuts. These small "Koupes" are offered at every kind of party, birthday parties, official receptions and various gatherings.

There are other kinds of "Koupes", such as the ones prepared like a pie in a dish and baked in the oven. But, according to my opinion the most original and tasty ones are the small size "Koupes" shaped by hand, one by one. So here is the recipe:

Ingredients for the paste:

2 kilos of fine ground wheat
1 tblsp of salt
3 cups of lukewarm water
½ cup of flour

Ingredients for the stuffing:

1 cup of parsley, finely cut
1 cup of vegetable oil
1 tsp of salt
1½ cups of onion cut into thick rings
½ kilo of minced meat
½ cup of pine-nuts
½ tsp of pepper

Three hours before you start preparing "Koupes", prepare the ground wheat paste. Put the ground wheat in a big wooden pot. Dissolve the salt in the lukewarm water and mix it in the wheat. Then sprinkle flour over the surface of the ground wheat, cover it with a thick serviette and leave it for 3 hours.

Then prepare the stuffing: Pour the oil into a wide frying pan and fry the onion slightly. Do the same with the parsley. Add the minced meat and stir for a while. Add the salt, and pepper, stir and cook the minced meat slowly until it is light brown. Put it in a strainer to drain the oil, and when cold add the pine nuts.

Stir the ground wheat and then knead it until a firm and smooth paste is formed. Take in your hands two tablespoons of the paste for the big size "Koupes" or one tablespoon for the small size "Koupes" and shape the paste into a ball. Using a special stick shape the paste into a tubular shape. Then, remove the stick carefully, stuff the "Koupa" with the stuffing and close its opening carefully. To shape them more easily, dip your hands into cold water every time you make one. In this way prepare all the "Koupes" and place them on a piece of wood sprinkled with flour.

Fry them in a deep frying pan with a lot of boiling oil. While they are being cooked turn them with a big spoon so that they get light brown on all sides. Put them in a strainer and then, on an absorbing paper. Serve them hot..

Maybe you will find the way of preparing them difficult. Maybe your first few attempts to shape the paste into tubular shapes will be a failure but with patience and practice you will finally succeed in making them.

Thus, you will acquire another good experience and you will proudly serve them to your family and friends as another delicacy. Good luck.

Makes 50—60 large size pieces or 100—120 small size pieces.

"KYPRIAKA LOUCANIKA" — CYPRUS SMOKED SAUSAGES

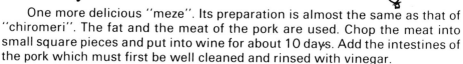

One more delicious "meze". Its preparation is almost the same as that of "chiromeri". The fat and the meat of the pork are used. Chop the meat into small square pieces and put into wine for about 10 days. Add the intestines of the pork which must first be well cleaned and rinsed with vinegar.

When the 10 days are over, take the meat out of the wine and sprinkle with salt, black pepper and crushed coriander. The intestines are filled with this meat and they are hung over the fireplace to be smoked and drained. They must be either kept hanging in a cool place or slightly fried and then put in clay jars, covered with melted pork fat. They are always served hot, cooked on charcoals or fried with eggs.

"OKTAPODHI KRASATO" — OCTOPUS IN WINE*

1 octopus (one or two kilos)
1 cup of olive oil
1 cup of dry red wine
1 piece of cinnamon
3 cloves of garlic
black pepper and salt to taste

For the octopus to be soft and well done, it must be well beaten and rubbed on a hard surface until it becomes white and its tantacles are swollen. At the same time the grease that covers it is removed too. After this is done, remove the eyes, the mouth and the intestines with a small sharp knife. Keep the ink that is found in the octopus to use it for cooking. Cut octopus into two inch pieces and put in the sausepan **without** any water on a low heat so that it rejects its own water. When there is little water left, add wine, olive oil and spices. Cover the saucepan and keep on cooking on a low heat for about 50—60 minutes until the octopus becomes very tender. When the stock is reduced, add 1—2 cups of water. It will be ready when there is a thick sauce in the pan. Serve with pilaff made with rice. It is an excellent "meze". May also be served cold.

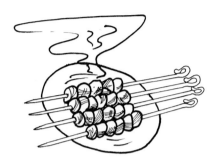

"SOUVLAKIA" —
GRILLED LAMB ON SKEWERS (KEBABS)

"Souvlakia" is again an excellent "meze" and goes well with "sheftalia". They are cooked in the same way as "sheftalia". In Cyprus, "souvlakia" are made of pork or lamb. However, the lamb's meat is more tasty and more nutritious. To be successful in cooking "souvlakia", one must remember two things: Firstly, to cook "souvlakia" slowly on red charcoal, which is spread apart so that low heat is emitted, and secondly to use the fat from the animal's tail, by putting some pieces among the pieces of meat. When the fat starts to melt, it is absorbed by the meat and at the same time it gives a nice aroma.

1 kilo of lamb's meat
1 tblsp of salt
1 cup of onions, finely chopped
2 lemons, cut in quarters
2 cups of yoghurt (plain)
2—3 tomatoes cut in big slices
2—3 cucumbers cut in big slices
½ kilo of lamb's tail fat
½ cup of parsley, finely chopped

Cut meat and fat in one-inch cubes and salt them. Pierce 4 pieces of meat and 3 pieces of fat alternately with each skewer. Cook on charcoal as mentioned above and serve hot. Put on each plate 1 tblsp of onion, 1 tsp of parsley, 1 tblsp of yoghurt, 1 quarter of lemon and pieces of tomatoes and cucumbers.

Makes 6—7 dishes.

23

"SKORDHOPSOMO" — GARLIC BREAD*

1 loaf of bread
4 cloves of garlic
½ cup of fresh butter or margarine

Cut the bread in thick slices. Crush the garlic until it becomes creamy, mix with butter and beat well. Spread the mixture on both sides of the bread slices, with a brush. Put the slices next to each other in order to reshape a loaf. Wrap them in foil and put in the oven (400°F) for 10 minutes approximately. Serve hot with almost all kinds of food.

Note: In Cypriot villages butter or margerine is not always used. Instead of butter, freshly squeezed olive oil (no more than a couple of days old) is used most often.

SOME MORE MEZEDHES COOKED ON CHARCOAL

The variety of the "mezedhes" offered in Cyprus is endless. As it was mentioned before, a "meze" can be made out of every kind of food. The most common of these have already been described. Before the subject of "mezedhes" is closed, some more "mezedhes" will be mentioned here, which are cooked on charcoal.

HALLOUMI : Cyprus goat milk cheese cut in slices, is placed on grill and cooked on charcoal.

PIGEONS : Young pigeons are cut in the middle so as to open up slightly but remain whole; they are salted, placed on grill and cooked on charcoal.

SMALL BIRDS-GAME : Whole as they are. Salted and passed through spits. Cooked for short time on charcoal.

CHICKEN LIVER : Cut into 2—3 pieces, salted and cooked on charcoal.

BLACK OLIVES : Placed on dense gridiron and cooked on charcoal.

LAMB'S PARTS : Lamb's liver, kidney, cuttlets and others are salted, placed on gridiron and cooked on charcoal.

"KYPRIAKES SOUPPES"
CYPRUS SOUPS

Cyprus soups are quite popular and can be served at all times of the day or night. They do not have to be served before meals. In the countryside, specially during the cold winter days, the farmers, shepherds, gardeners and workers have a hot soup for their breakfast. They even add some hot red pepper to it so that it becomes even hotter. Some of them drink "zivania" with their soup, a spirit made by the distillation of grapes.

Cyprus soups are purely national and are prepared and served in the same way as they were served hundreds of years ago. The ingredients used are either cereals or Cypriot milk products such as "trachanas" and "halloumi".

The main Cypriot soup is "trachanas", "Avgolemoni" followed by lentils-soup, "louvana", "psarosoupa", and so on.

25

"PSAROSOUPA" — FISH SOUP

1½ kilos of small sea fish
1 cup of carrots cut into small pieces
1 cup of onions, finely chopped
1 cup of ripe sieved tomatoes
2 tblsps of olive oil
½ cup of diced potatoes
¼ cup of lemon juice
½ cup of rice
¼ cup of parsley, finely chopped
Salt and pepper to taste

Clean the fish and wash well. Put the fish in a pan containing about 3 litres of cold water and boil. Pass through thin sieve and put the broth back in the pan. Add the vegetables and let them cook. Bone the fish and add to the pan with the rice. When the rice is cooked add tomatoes, olive oil, salt and pepper. Five minutes later remove the pan from the heat. Add lemon juice, stir and serve. Garnish each plate with parsley.

Makes 6—8 dishes.

"SOUPA LOUVANA" — YELLOW PEA SOUP

The yellow pea soup is served during the fasting days. It is also cooked at every other time of the year because of its great popularity, with one difference; instead of using water, yellow peas are cooked with broth made from legs of beef or any other strong broth. In both cases the ingredients are the same.

10 cups of broth or water
2 cups of yellow peas
1 cup of onions, finely chopped
5—6 peppercorns
5—6 black olives for each person
½ cup of rice
¼ cup of olive oil and
¼ cup of cornoil mixed
½ cup of lemon juice
Salt to taste

Wash yellow peas well. Pour them in a deep pan and add cold water or meat broth. Heat and when boiling reduce heat and simmer for about 45 minutes until cooked. In the meantime skim the soup for 2—3 times. Then add rice and let cook for another 15 minutes. Ten minutes before removing the pan from the heat, fry the onions in mixed oil until light brown and add them with the oil into the soup. Pour the lemon juice, stir and serve at once. On each plate of soup drop 5—6 black olives.

Makes 4—5 dishes.

"FAGGI KSIDHATI" — LENTIL SOUP WITH VINEGAR*

A national soup which is usually prepared during fasting days.

1 cup of lentils
1 cup of spring onions, finely chopped
1 cup of coriander leaves, finely chopped
1 cup of lettuce, finely chopped
3 cloves of garlic
1 tblsp of flour
½ cup of wine vinegar
Salt and pepper to taste

Wash the lentils well and put them in a deep pan of cold water, on low heat for about 45 minutes. Then add garlic and the thinly chopped vegetables. Simmer the soup for another 20 minutes. In a bowl of hot water dissolve the flour and gradually pour it back to the pan while stirring. Add vinegar, salt and pepper, heat for 5 more minutes, and serve the soup hot.

Makes 4—6 dishes.

"SOUPPA TRACHANAS" —
SOUP WITH CRUSHED WHEAT DRIED IN YOGHOURT

"Trachanas" soup is the national soup of Cyprus. It is quite nutritious and well-known to everybody. Tourists who tasted it, have enjoyed it as much as the Cypriots.

Before going into preparation of "trachanas" soup I will give you some further information about "trachanas" which is the main constituent of this soup. "Trachanas" is a mixture of crushed wheat and yoghourt which when cooked, becomes a thick paste. Then, this paste is cut into small but long pieces with the sharp edge of a wide knife which is dipped each time into cold water. These pieces are then placed on wooden trays in rows. Each piece must be well apart from the other. They are left in the sun for about 4—5 days until they dry. These pieces of "trachanas" are kept into dry glass or clay jars to be used especially in the cold winter nights.

You can buy "trachanas" from grocery shops. It is sold in airtight bags or in jars.

The "trachanas" soup is easily made and is prepared as follows:

> 6 cups of chicken broth
> 1 cup of diced halloumi
> ½ kilo of "trachanas"
> ¼ cup of lemon juice
> Salt and pepper to taste

Soak the "trachanas" in cold water for about one hour. Then drain and put in a pan which contains the cold chicken broth. Leave for about one hour on low heat, until it becomes quite a thick soup. While on the heat stir every 10 minutes so that it does not stick to the pan. five minutes before the pan is removed from the fire, add lemon juice and halloumi. Serve the soup hot.

Makes 6—8 dishes

"KHORTOSOUPPA" — VEGETABLE SOUP

10 cups of broth made from chicken
   or any other meat
1 cup of diced potatoes
1 cup of diced carrots
1 cup of celery, finely chopped
1 cup of diced small zucchini
1 cup of ripe tomatoes, cut in big
   pieces
4—5 peppercorns hot
  (if soup preferred hot)
½ cup of onions, finely chopped
¼ cup of rice
½ cup of lemon juice
Salt to taste

    Boil broth and add the thinly chopped vegetables (except the tomatoes and potatoes) and let cook. Then add the potatoes, tomatoes, rice, salt and peppercorns. Let cook for another 15 minutes. Serve hot in warm bowls. In each bowl add a few drops of lemon juice.

Makes 6—8 dishes

Note: Vegetable soup may be prepared with water instead of broth. If done so, add ¼ cup of olive oil and ¾ cup of corn oil when the rice and tomatoes are added.

"SOUPPA PATCHIA" — LAMB'S OR CALF'S HEAD SOUP*

This is a very nutritious and popular soup. It is usually served at restaurants after midnight, to people who come from the cinema, theatre or cabaret. The original recipe for "patchia" specifies that it must be prepared from the various parts of the calf's head, such as brain, eyes, tongue, sweetbread and meat. For this reason only a few restaurants make the original soup. Most of the restaurants make it out of lamb's head because it is lighter for the stomach. The housewife does the same because it is impossible to use a calf's head for only a small family. So, in spite of the fact that "patchia" made out of calf is more nutritious and tastier, I shall present the more common "patchia" using a lamb's head.

1 lamb's head
10—12 cups of water
1 bay leaf
1 whole medium-sized onion
3 cloves of garlic, well crushed
1 carrot, well-cleaned
1 stalk celery, cut into 3 pieces
2 small ripe tomatoes (uncut)
6—8 slices of toast cut in halves
1 cup of wine vinegar
Salt to taste.

For the sauce:

2 tblsps of flour
2 tblsps butter
3 eggs
2 tblsps of lemon juice
Salt and pepper

Wash the head and put in a pan of cold water. When it starts to boil remove the foam from the top. Do this two or three times. Add celery, onion, carrots, bay leaf, salt and tomatoes (piercing them with a fork on opposite sides). Simmer the head until the meat may be separated from the bones. Pass the broth through sieve and put it in a small pan over low heat to keep it hot. Take the brain out carefully and cut it into slices. Do the same with the tongue and the rest of the head. Beat the garlic together with the vinegar in a bowl and keep aside. Heat the butter in a frying pan and add the flour to it, little by little, beating it at the same time. Then add some of the broth until the mixture is quite thick and remove from heat. Beat the eggs well with lemon juice and add to the frying pan. Stir and simmer the sauce for five minutes and transfer into a small saucepan to keep warm. When serving put two pieces of toast into each soup plate. Then put the various kinds of meat and cover with the broth. Add a spoonful of the vinegar and garlic mixture and add 2—3 tblsps of the sauce. In the middle of the plate put one or two slices of brain and serve at once.

Makes 6—8 dishes.

"SOUPPA AVGOLEMONO" — RICE SOUP WITH EGG-AND-LEMON SAUCE

This is a famous and very popular soup that is as tasty as nutritious.

8 cups of chicken broth
1 cup of rice
6 egg yolks
½ cup of lemon juice
Salt and pepper to taste.

Cook the rice in broth and remove the pan from heat. Beat the egg yolks together with the lemon juice. Gradually add to the yolks 1—2 cups of broth from the pan, keeping on beating. Pour the egg mixture gradually back into the soup, and stir. Add salt and pepper. Heat the soup well and serve.

Makes 6—8 dishes.

"YIOUVARLAKIA SOUPPA" — SOUP WITH MEATBALLS*

1 clove of garlic, finely chopped
1 tblsp onion, finely chopped
1 egg
1 tsp of parsley
8 cups of chicken broth
2 egg yolks
½ kilo of minced meat
½ cup of rice
½ cup of flour
Juice of 2 lemons
Salt to taste.

Put the minced meat into a bowl and add garlic, onion, egg, parsley and half of the rice. Knead well. Form into small balls and sprinkle with flour. Put the broth in a pan and heat well. Add the meat balls in it, as well as the rest of the rice. Simmer for about 30 minutes until they are cooked. Beat the eggs well together with the lemon juice and then add 2 cups of broth from the pan little by little and keep on beating at the same time. Pour the egg mixture back into the pan and add salt. Let the soup boil for about 5 minutes.

In each plate serve some soup with 4—5 meat balls "yiouvarlakia".

Makes 6—8 dishes.

"SOUPPA HOUMMI" — CHICK PEA SOUP*

Even though "hoummi" originated in the Middle East, it is enjoyed by Cypriots, and like "patshia soup", is served in restaurants especially to the "night customers". It is quite a warming and nutritious soup because its main constituents are chick peas and "tachini". It is also very tasty and appetizing, so we present it to you, hoping that you will like it.

2½ cups of chick peas
4 tblsps of "tachine"
(you may find it at any grocery store,
under this name)
3 cloves of crushed garlic
6—8 black olives for each person
1 tblsp of salt for the sauce
1 tblsp of salt for the boiling
of the chick peas
50 pieces of bread (1 inch square each)
½ tsp of hot red pepper
½ cup of lemon juice
½ cup of parsley, finely chopped
½ cup of olive oil

Soak the chick peas over night. The next day, wash them and put them into a pan with cold water and salt. Let boil for about one and a half hour until the peas are soft. Pass through sieve and keep the broth hot. Put the chick peas into a mixer and mix until they become a soft cream. Put the salt, garlic, "tachini" and lemon juice into a bowl and stir a little; add them to the chick peas, in the mixer, and mix. Then pour broth in the chick peas, little by little until the mixture is quite thin. Put the pieces of bread into 6—8 bowls and cover them with the chick pea mixture. Garnish with the parsley, olive oil, olives and some pepper.

Makes 6—8 dishes.

"ZIMARIKA" — PASTAS

"KYPRIAKA LAZANIA" — CYPRUS LASAGNA

4 cups of flour
4 eggs
1 tsp of salt
1 cup of grated cheese
3 cups of fresh milk

Pass flour through a sieve and add salt. Make a small hole in the middle of the flour and break the eggs into it. Knead adding one cup of milk gradually until the dough is quite hard. Cover with a thick cloth for ½ — 1 hour. Cut the dough in small pieces and roll into thin sheets. Let the sheets dry and put 2 to 4 on top each other. Cut the edges and then cut in small squares of 8—10 cm each side. Spread them well apart onto a lightly floured pan, and let them dry completely. It would be even better if they stayed there for a whole day. Boil water with salt and add "Lazania". Stir so that they do not stick together. Boil for 7—10 minutes and drain most of the water. Keep about 2 cups of water in the pan with the "Lazania" and add the two cups of milk. Lower the heat and simmer for about 5—6 minutes to absorb the milk. On a big plate sprinkle some grated cheese and spread a layer of "Lazania". Sprinkle some more cheese on "Lazania" and make another layer. Continue until all "Lazania" is used. If preferred, tomato sauce may be added on "Lazania". Here is the recipe.

For tomato sauce:
1 kilo of ripe tomatoes, peeled
1 tblsp of onion, thinly chopped
1 tblsp of parsley, thinly chopped
1 tblsp of celery
1 bayleaf

1 tsp of sugar
1 tsp of salt
½ tsp of pepper
½ cup of corn oil

Put onion in a small pan of heated oil until golden. Add parsley and celery until lightly cooked. Cut tomatoes in small pieces and add them to the pan, together with the bayleaf, sugar, salt and pepper. Stir with a wooden spoon. Cover pan and cook on low heat for about 35—40 minutes. Serve hot on top of Lasagna. If there is some sauce left, you can keep it in the refrigerator for about a week.

Makes 6—8 dishes.

"BOUREKIA ME KIMA"
PASTRIES STUFFED WITH MINCED MEAT

For stuffing:

2 eggs
1 tblsp of finely chopped onions
1 tblsp of chopped parsley
1 tblsp of tomato paste
1½ cup of minced lamb
½ cup of corn oil
½ cup of grated cheese
½ cup of hot water
Salt and pepper

For dough:

3 cups of plain flour
½ cup of corn oil
½ cup of cold water
½ tsp of salt

First make the stuffing: Heat oil in frying pan and fry the onion until tender. Add minced meat, stir well and cook until light brown. Dissolve tomato paste in ½ cup of hot water and pour in the pan. Add parsley, salt and pepper, reduce heat and simmer gently until all juice is absorbed. Remove pan from heat and when cool add first the eggs, and then the cheese. Mix well until stuffing becomes soft.

Then make dough:

Sift flour and mix with the salt. Make a hollow in flour and pour the oil. Using your fingers mix well until oil is absorbed. Gradually add water and knead to firm dough. Shape dough into a ball, cover with a thick cloth and leave to rest for one hour. Knead again for another 5 minutes and divide in three equal portions. Roll out each portion of pastry to make a long wide and thin sheet. With a pastry cutter cut the pastry in small rounds of 3 inch diameter each. Brush lightly with cold water round the edge of pastry. Place a tablespoonful of stuffing in the centre, fold over and press edges with a fork to seal well. Fry "bourekia" in deep pan in very hot oil for about 3 minutes or until golden. Drain on paper towel and serve hot.

Makes 20—25 pieces

"LAZANIA STO FOURNO" — OVEN BAKED CYPRUS LASAGNA

For the cream:

3 cups of fresh milk
4 tblsps of oil
4 tblsps of flour
4 egg yolks
1 cup of grated cheese
¼ tsp of nutmeg
Salt and pepper

For the minced meat sauce:

1 tblsp of onion, thinly chopped
1 cup ripe tomatoes, thinly chopped
1 tsp tomato purée
½ cup of corn oil
1 kilo of minced meat
½ cup of parsley, thinly chopped
½ cup of dry white wine
Salt and pepper

For the dough:

4 cups of flour
4 eggs
1 cup of fresh milk
1 tsp of salt

Preparation of dough:

Pass flour through sieve and add salt. Gradually add eggs and milk mixing them well until the dough becomes quite stiff. Cover with a thick cloth and leave for about ½—1 hour. Cut into small pieces and pass them through a machine to shape them into long strips, 14 cm in width. Place 2—3 of these strips, one on top of the other and cut with a knife starting with the edges so that they are straight, and then cutting in the middle. Cut again in squares 7 cm wide. Spread them well apart and sprinkle with flour.

Preparation of cream:

Heat oil in a small pan and gradually add flour while stirring. Add milk (quite hot) little by little and keep on stirring. When it is quite thick remove pan from heat and mix with the egg yolks, the grated cheese, the nutmeg, salt and pepper.

35

Preparation of meat sauce:

Heat oil in a frying pan and add onions until they are light brown. Add meat and stir until it is light brown. Add wine and when it has boiled for two minutes, add the parsley, the chopped tomatoes and the tomato purée. Lower heat and cook for about 30 minutes.

Final preparation of "Lasagna"

Heat the "lasagna" in boiling water for 5—7 minutes and drain. Butter a pie-dish and place a layer of "lasagna". Cover with cream and then with the meat sauce. Sprinkle with grated cheese and repeat twice more. Cover the top of the third layer with the rest of the white cream. Sprinkle with grated cheese and with a few drops of oil. Put pie-dish in oven (medium) for half an hour or until the cream is light brown. Remove pie-dish from oven and while still warm cut into squares. Serve hot.

Makes 6—8 dishes

Note: In some Cypriot villages instead of using minced meat, they use Cyprus sausages in the "lazania". After removing the skin from sausages they cut them into small pieces and they become like minced meat. This is because minced meat is not easily found in the villages and especially because the sausages give a special taste and aroma to "lazania".

"KALOYIRKA" —
CYPRUS PASTRIES STUFFED WITH MINCED MEAT

The dough:
4 cups of sifted flour
4 eggs
1 cup of fresh milk
1 tsp of salt

The Stuffing:
1½ cup of minced veal
1 tblsp of finely chopped onions
1 tblsp of chopped parsley
1 cup of hot water
½ cup of corn oil
Salt and pepper

The Sauce:
1 kilo of peeled ripe tomatoes
1 tblsp of finely chopped onions
1 tblsp of finely chopped parsley
1 tblsp of finely chopped celery
1 bayleaf
1 tsp of sugar
1 tsp of salt
½ tsp of pepper
½ cup of corn oil

Put salt into the flour, add eggs and stir. Pour milk and mix it. Knead until dough is quite firm. Cover with a thick dry towel and let stand for ½—1 hour. Cut dough into small pieces and roll thin (⅛ inch) sheets of about 4—5 inches wide. The length is not important.

Now prepare stuffing. Put onions in heated oil. Add parsley and then the minced meat. Stir for 1—2 minutes and add water, salt and pepper. Lower heat and let meat cook until it becomes light brown in colour and absorbs the water.

The sauce is prepared as follows: Heat oil in a small pan and put the onions into it. Then, add celery and parsley. When they are heated add the finely chopped tomatoes. Add salt, pepper, sugar and bayleaf. Stir well. Lower heat and cook the tomatoes for about 30 minutes.

Put a tea spoonful of stuffing into the middle of a strip of flattened dough. Each pile of stuffing must be 2 to 3 inches apart and centered on the strip. Fold the strip length so as to cover the stuffing. Press the sides together with the edge of your palm, flatten the areas between the pile of stuffing. Now with a large tumbler glass cut the dough around each mound so that you are left with half-moon shapes. Be careful not to cut the folded edge of the dough.

Heat water with salt in a big pan. When the water is boiling put a small number of "Kaloyrka" into it, to be cooked for about 7 minutes. The process is repeated for each dozen or so "Kaloyrka". The water must be boiling every time some more "Kaloyrka" are added into the pan.

Remove with a large draining spoon and put into a platter. Cover with the tomato sauce, and serve hot.   Makes 8—10 dishes

37

"MAKARONIA TOU FOURNOU" — OVEN BAKED MACARONI WITH LAYERS OF MINCED MEAT

For the macaroni:

1 kilo of thick macaroni
  (the heaviest grade of spaghetti available)
1 cup of grated cheese
1 tblsp of salt
2 tblsps of oil
¼ tsp of dry mint
¼ tsp of cinnamon
¼ tsp of pepper

For the cream:

5 cups of fresh milk
3 tblsps of flour
3 tblsps of butter
4 egg yolks
½ cup of grated cheese
¼ tsp of nutmeg
Salt and pepper

For the minced meat:

1 tblsp of onions, finely chopped
1 tblsp of parsley, finely chopped
1 cup of ripe tomatoes, finely chopped
1 tsp of tomato purée
¾ kilo of minced meat (beef and pork mixed)
½ cup of dry white wine
½ cup of corn oil
Salt and pepper

Firstly, prepare the minced meat mixture. Heat oil in a frying pan and add the onions. Then, add the meat and stir until it is light brown. Pour the wine and when it boils add parsley, tomatoes, salt, pepper and tomato purée. Stir, lower the heat and simmer for about 30 minutes. In the meantime prepare the cream. Heat milk until it boils. Heat oil in a different pan and add flour to it slowly. Stir constantly with an egg wisk until this mixture is thick and smooth. Then immediately add the hot milk, again little by little and stirring at the same time, until it becomes a smooth cream. Remove pan from heat and add the egg yolks, the grated cheese, the nutmeg, salt and pepper. Now prepare the macaroni. Boil water and add salt, oil and then macaroni. Cook for about 6—8 minutes and stir two or three times, so that they do not stick. Drain and put in a large bowl. Add pepper, mint, cinnamon and 3 tblsps of your cream preparation and mix well. Cover a baking tray with butter and put in it a thick layer or macaroni. Sprinkle with grated cheese and cover with half of the cream. Add the meat and the rest of the macaroni on top. Cover with the rest of the cream and sprinkle with grated cheese. Put in the oven (600°) for about 10 minutes or until it is light brown. Take the baking tray out of the oven and when it is cooled cut into squares. It can be served hot or cold.

Makes 12—15 pieces.

"KYPRIAKES RAVIOLES" — CYPRUS RAVIOLI

For dough:
3 cups of plain flour
3 eggs
1 cup of cold water
1 tsp of salt

For stuffing:
1½ cup of grated halloumi cheese
1½ tsps of dry mint
3 eggs

For garnish:
1 cup of grated halloumi cheese
1 tsp of dry mint
½ cup of melted butter
Chicken broth to cook ravioli

Sift flour and mix the salt. Make a hollow in flour and break the eggs. Mix with the flour while gradually adding water until it becomes a soft dough. Knead for about 10 minutes to be smooth and elastic, and make a ball. Sprinkle some flour and cover with a thick cloth to rest for one hour.

In a bowl pour the grated halloumi cheese, add eggs, dry mint and mix well to become a thick mixture. Knead dough for another 5 minutes and divide in four equal portions. Roll out each portion to become a long thin strip 3 inches wide. Place a teaspoonful of cheese mixture at every 2 inches interval on the centre of the strip. With a brush dipped in water moisten lightly the strip around one side of the stuffing. Fold pastry over stuffing. Press well between the mounds of stuffing and along the edges. Cut ravioli in half-moon shape with the rim of a water glass. With the tines of a fork press the edges of ravioli to seal well. Place ravioli on a cloth and repeat to make ravioli with the remaining ingredients. In a deep saucepan of boiling salted chicken broth cook ravioli 10—15 pieces each time for about 15—20 minutes until tender. Strain ravioli and put in a platter. Pour over them some melted butter and sprinkle with a lot of halloumi and mint mixture. Serve hot.

Makes 6—8 dishes

"KOLOKOTES" — PASTRIES STUFFED WITH PUMPKIN

"Kolokotes" are very popular in Cyprus. They are usually eaten during the cold winter days when people need a quick hot breakfast or even when they want to avoid eating eggs and smoked meats. "Kolokotes" are as I believe unknown outside the island. However, they are so tasty and nutritious that it is worth trying them. You must remember that the stuffing of "kolokotes" must be prepared 24 hours in advance.

For the stuffing:
- 3 cups of diced red sweet pumpkin
- 3 tblsps of pourgouri (crushed wheat)
- 3 tblsps of corn oil
- 2 tblsps of sugar
- 1 cup of sultana raisins
- 1 tsp of cinnamon powder
- ½ tsp of salt
- ½ tsp of pepper
- ½ tsp of pounded cloves

For the dough :
- 4 cups of plain flour
- 1 tblsp of lemon juice
- 1 tsp of salt
- ½ cup of corn oil
- ½ cup of water.

Mix all stuffing ingredients in a glass bowl and let stay for 24 hours. The next day prepare the dough: Sift the flour and mix with the salt. Make a small hollow in flour and pour in the oil. Using your fingers mix well until the oil is absorbed throughout. Add lemon juice and water little by little and knead to become one firm dough. Cover with a thick cloth, and leave it to rest for about 45 minutes. Then knead another 5 minutes and cut into 6—8 round balls. Roll each ball to make a long and wide sheet about ⅛ of inch thick. Cut the sheets into a round shape about 6 inches diameter. Brush lightly with cold water over the flattened dough. Place 1½ tblsps of stuffing in the middle and fold to get the shape of half moon. With the tines of fork press the edges of "kolokotes" to seal well.

Place "kolokotes" in a greased baking tray and bake them in hot oven for 20—25 minutes or until they are light brown. Serve hot.

Makes about 25 pieces.

"ELIOTI" — OVEN BAKED OLIVE BREAD

4 cups of flour
1½ cup of olive oil
3 tsps of baking powder
1 cup of evaporated milk
1½ cup of black olives without
    their stones and finely chopped
½ cup of chopped onions
1 tsp of mint powder

Mix flour with baking powder and mint. Heat oil in a frying pan and put the onions and the olives in it, until they are light brown. Let cool and empty the contents of the frying pan into the flour. Knead well. Add milk and knead again. Cover with a thick towel and leave it for one hour. Butter a bread pan, put the dough in it. Bake in oven (medium) 350°F for about an hour. Serve it hot or cold.   Makes 12—15 pieces

"PITTA" — FLAT (ENVELOPE) BREAD

"Pitta" is a kind of flat small bread, that when cooked separates into two, like an envelope. It is mainly used for putting in it kebab, sheftalia, grilled sausages or pastourma and also replace ordinary bread.

4   cups hard flour
1 1/2 cups warm water
1   teaspoon salt
1   teaspoon dry east

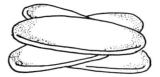

— Mix flower with salt, sift and
    separate one cup of it
— In a bowl dissolve east in warm water,
    blend in one cup of flour to make a thick liquid, cover and leave in a warm place for 15 minutes until frothy. Blend in frothy liquid remaining flour and knead to make a thick dough. Shape dough into a ball, sprinkle on top little flour, cover with a cloth and leave for 30 minutes to rise. Knead dough for 2-3 minutes, divide into 10-12 equal pieces and shape them into flat oval form. Cover "pitta" with a cloth and leave them for another 30 minutes. Heat oven to get hot and place in it a heavy baking sheet for 15 minutes. Grease baking sheet with oil and place on it the flat breads. Bake breads in a very hot oven for about 4 minutes until pitta puffs, turn them and bake another 3 minutes and remove them from oven. Before using put pitta on charcoal where you grille kebab to get hot and slightly brown. Using a knife cut one side of pitta to open and put kebab in it.

Makes 10-12 "pitta"

"PILAFIA" — PILAFFS

Pilaffs are well-known in Cyprus, and are well liked by the people, especially Villagers in the countryside who usually eat them during the gathering of the grapes, carobs, wheat and olives.

Because the farmers are in the fields all day the dish is often eaten cold. They can be accompanied by black olives, smoked herrings, various assorted dried meats, cheeses or even vegetables.

"PILAFI POURGOURI" — CRUSHED WHEAT PILAF

2 cups of pourgouri (crushed wheat)
3 cups of chicken broth
1 cup of peeled tomatoes, finely chopped
½ cup of corn oil
½ cup of onions, finely chopped
¾ cup of vermicelli noodles
Salt and pepper.

Heat the oil in a deep pan, add onions and vermicelly and fry gently. Add the chicken broth and leave until boiling. Wash very fast pourgouri in a sieve under running water and pour in the pan. Add tomatoes, salt pepper and stir. When it starts to boil again, reduce heat, cover the pan and simmer for 25—30 minutes, until all broth is absorbed. Remove pan from the heat, take off the cover, put on the rims of the pan a thick towel and put back the cover. Leave for 10 minutes to absorb the vapors. Serve pilafi hot, and in each plate put 2 table spoonfull of yoghurt.

Makes 5—7 dishes

"MOUTCHENTRA" — LENTIL AND RICE PILAFF

2 cups of lentils
1 cup of rice
1½ cup of onions cut in thin rings
¾ cup of olive oil
6 cups of cold water
Salt and pepper to taste.

Soak the lentils all through the night. Cook lentils for about 15 minutes in a pan of water and salt. Add the rice and cook for 15 more minutes, on low heat, until the water is absorbed. Ten minutes before the pan is removed from heat cover it with a thick cloth and with its own cover on top of the cloth; thus keeping the rice moist and fluffy. Heat oil in a frying pan and fry the onions until they are light brown. Empty the contents of the frying pan (oil and onions) in the pan containing the pilaff. Some people add 1 cup of bread cut into small cubes into the frying pan together with the onions. The pilaff is now ready to eat. Serve hot with the crisp onions covering the pilaff.

Makes 6—8 dishes

"SPANACHORIZO" — RICE PILAFF WITH SPINACH

1 kilo of fresh spinach
1 cup of rice
2 cups of water
½ cup of oil
½ cup of onions, finely chopped
Salt and pepper to taste

Clean spinach and wash well. Cut into small pieces. In a deep saucepan fry the onions. Add the spinach and dry it until it softens. Pour in water and add salt and pepper. Cover pan and cook spinach for about 35 minutes. Add rice, stir and let cook for 20 more minutes or until the water is absorbed. As a reminder: 10 minutes before the pan is removed from heat, cover with a thick cloth in order to help keep the rice fluffy.

Makes 5—7 dishes

"PILAFI RIZI" — RICE PILAFF

2 cups of rice
4 cups of chicken or any other kind
   of meat broth
½ cup of onions, finely chopped
¼ cup of lemon juice
1 cup of ripe tomatoes, finely chopped
½ cup of corn oil
Salt and pepper to taste

Pour the oil in a saucepan and fry the onion. Add the rice, stir for a while so that it whitens, add the lemon juice, salt and pepper. Then, add the tomatoes, stir for a while and finally add the broth. Cover the saucepan and cook the rice for about 15—20 minutes.

Put the saucepan away from the fire and remove the lid. Cover the opening of the saucepan with a thick serviette, put the lid on top of it and leave for about 10 minutes so that the serviette absorbs the steam of the pilaff. Serve while hot.

Makes 6—7 dishes

Note: This kind of pilaff is served either alone as a main dish or as a side dish accompanying meat or fish cooked in sauce.

"YIOUVETSI" — OVEN BAKED MACARONI WITH LAMB MEAT

1 kilo of lamb cut in cubes (4 cm).
3 cups of "kritharaki" (Type of noodle in rice shape)
1 cup of grated cheese
1 cup of hot meat broth
1 cup of ripe tomatoes, finely chopped
½ cup of tomato purée
½ cup of cornoil
Salt and pepper to taste

Fry onion in a saucepan until soft. Add meat and stir until light brown. Dissolve the tomato purée in a cup of hot broth and pour in the pan. Add chopped tomatoes, salt and pepper and stir. Cover the pan and simmer the meat for one hour. Twenty minutes before removing the pan from the heat, prepare "kritharaki" pasta. In a pan with boiling salted water pour "kritharaki" to boil just for 10 minutes, and drain them. Empty the contents of the saucepan (meat and its sauce) in a medium size "yiouvetsi" (a clay pot). Pour "kritharaki" pasta on top of the meat. Stir to mix pasta and meat and put in oven on high heat to bake for 20 minutes. Serve "yiouvetsi" hot and sprinkle with a lot of grated cheese.

Makes 6—8 dishes

Note: If a "yiouvetsi" pot is not available then use a deep ovenproof dish. The deeper the dish the better the meal.

"RESSI" — CYPRUS WHEAT PILAFF

"Ressi" is a kind of Cyprus pilaff which has been served for hundreds of years. It is considered as a National food. It is made on special occasions; especially at wedding receptions, in the countryside, where all of the old customs are kept devotedly. It is something unusual for a wedding to take place without the presentation of "ressi". The countrymen, have a saying about this, which says that "a wedding without 'ressi' is like winter without rain".

A great importance is given to its preparation and all the rules are kept with great detail. The washing and crushing of the wheat is usually the younger girl's job, and it is accompanied by music made with traditional musical instruments. Its cooking needs not only a lot of patience, as it requires at least 5—6 hours, but also a lot of expertise. The ingredients consist of, lamb's meat, wheat and the fat from the animal's tail. The preparation is given below. The proportions given below are for a maximum of one hundred people. — "Ressi" is served in cups.

6 kilos of lamb	7 kilos of wheat
6 kilos of fat from the animal's tail	1 cup of salt

Remove the small stones or any small pieces of wood from the wheat and wash in a lot of cold water. Put in a big jar and cover with water (3 times as much as the weight of the wheat) and let it soak for about 4 hours. Drain and spread on cloths in the sun until it is completely dry. Break it lightly. Cut meat into big pieces and put in a big pot. Add water (3 times the weight of the meat). Add salt and cook on high heat until the bones can be separated from the meat. Pass through sieve and keep the broth; remove the bones and cut the meat into small pieces. Cut also, the fat into small pieces. In a big pot add the meat, the fat and the broth and boil for about half an hour. Then add the wheat. Lower the heat, to medium, and cook the "ressi" for about 5 hours or until it becomes a thick paste. Stir slowly, from time to time with a big wooden spoon. At intervals, add more water, because the wheat absorbs it. It is not unusual to need 6 more litres of water. Serve "ressi" hot, with a small spoon.

Note: The traditional recipe is given here but smaller amounts can be made by proportionately reducing the ingredients.

"KYPRIAKES SALATES"
CYPRUS SALADS

In Cyprus there are abundant vegetables for salads and they can be found all through the year.

In the market people can find tomatoes, cucumbers, lettuce, celery, cabbages, dill, green-fresh onions, coriander, parsley, mint, zuchini, potatoes, cauliflower, beets, eggplant, wild plants found on the mountains and other.

If we were to present all of the various combinations we would have hundreds of salads.

However, we shall refer to only a few of them; the most common in Cyprus.

"SALATA KOUKIA FRESKA
GREEN BROAD BEANS SALAD

1 kilo fresh green broad beans
3 gloves garlic
3 stalks of fresh fennel
½ cup of olive oil
¼ cup of vinegar
Salt to taste

String all the beans and keep but the tenderest shells. Put them in a pan of boiling salted water for about 40 minutes. Strain and put them in a bowl. Crush the garlic with the salt and mix into the beans. Beat olive oil and vinegar and pour over the beans. On top sprinkle the finely chopped fennel. Serve cold garnished with few black olives.

For 4—6 persons.

"SALATA KHORIATIKI" — VILLAGE SALAD

10 black olives
2 stalks of celery
1 green pepper
½ kilo of tomatoes
½ kilo of cucumbers
½ a lettuce
¼ cup of onions, finely chopped
½ cup of "fetta" cheese, broken
   into small bits
½ cup of small eggplants, finely
   chopped
½ cup of pickled caper
½ cup of olive oil
½ cup of vinegar
Salt to taste

   Wash all vegetables well and chop them into pieces. Cut tomatoes in eighths. Put in a salad bowl and mix. Sprinkle first the olives and then the pickled caper over the salad. On the very top add the "fetta" cheese and pour beaten oil with vinegar over the salad.

For 8—10 persons.

"TOMATOSALATA" — TOMATO SALAD

1 kilo of tomatoes
1 big onion
¼ kilo of cucumbers
½ cup of olive oil
½ cup of vinegar
½ tsp of mint powder
Salt and pepper

   Wash tomatoes, cut in big slices and put in two rows in the salad bowl. Peel cucumbers and cut into slices. Place around the tomatoes. Cut onion in rings and sprinkle on the surface of the salad. Mix olive oil and vinegar, salt and pepper in a bowl and beat them well. Pour over salad. Finally sprinkle the mint powder.

For 4—6 persons.

47

"SALATA TIS LAMBRIS" — EASTER SALAD

This salad is mostly prepared on Easter day and the following days. It consists of green onions that are abundant in the season and of hard boiled eggs.

1 lettuce
10 green leaves of spring onions
3 hard-boiled eggs
½ cup of olive oil
½ cup of vinegar
Salt and pepper

Wash the onions and lettuce, and cut into big pieces. Cut the hard-boiled eggs in big pieces and mix all the ingredients together. Beat olive oil and vinegar with salt and pepper and pour over salad.

For 4—6 persons.

"SALATA KHORTA VRASTA" — BOILED VEGETABLE SALAD

2 medium-sized potatoes
2 small zucchini
2 carrots
1 small piece of cauliflower
2 hard-boiled eggs
1 tblsp of parsley, finely chopped
½ cup of olive oil
½ cup of lemon juice
Salt and pepper

Clean vegetables and wash. Put them all, except the cauliflower, in a pot of boiling salted water. Let cook for about 20 minutes. The cauliflower is cooked alone, in a small pan in which a piece of bread is added. Beat olive oil and lemon juice together. Cut the hard-boiled eggs into very tiny pieces and mix with parsley. Drain boiled vegetables and put in a platter. Pour the beaten olive oil and lemon juice over the vegetables and sprinkle with the tiny pieces of the eggs. Can be served hot as well as cold.

For 4—6 persons.

"SALATA KOKKINOGOULIA" — BEETROOT SALAD*

3 stalks of fresh celery, finely
   chopped
3 cloves of garlic, finely chopped
10 springs of parsley, finely
   chopped
3 tblsps of olive oil
2 tblsps of vinegar
½ kilo of beetroot
¼ kilo of potatoes
Salt and pepper

Wash beetroot and put in a pan with cold water and salt, to be cooked. Do the same with potatoes in a different pan. After they are cooked, peel them and cut into quite big slices. Put in a row in a salad plate. Next add a row of parsley and a row of celery. Sprinkle garlic all over the salad. Pour beaten olive oil and vinegar over them. Add salt and pepper to taste.

For 4—6 persons.

"SALATA DHIAFORA KHORTA" — MIXED VEGETABLE SALAD

1 radish (see note)
2 green peppers
2 fresh onions
3 stalks of lettuce
3 stalks of fresh celery
1 small cucumber
10—12 black olives
½ bunch of mint
½ bunch of coriander
½ cup of olive oil
½ cup of vinegar
Salt and pepper

Clean vegetables, wash well, drain and cut them into small pieces. Mix them all and put them in the salad bowl. Put olives on top. Beat olive oil, salt, pepper and vinegar. Pour over salad.

For 4—6 persons.

Note: In Cyprus a radish grows as long and thick as a big carrot.

49

"PSARIKA"
FISH AND SEA FOOD

"PSARI STO FOURNO" — OVEN BAKED FISH*

1½ kilo of fish (small ones or a big
    one)
1 cup of carrots cut in thin slices
1 cup of onions cut in thin slices
1 cup of olive oil
1 cup of celery, finely chopped
1 cup of parsley, finely chopped
3 cloves of garlic, finely chopped
2 bay leaves
2 cups of ripe tomatoes, finely
    chopped
1 tblsp of tomato purée
1½ kilo of potatoes cut in slices
⅛ tsp of oregano
Salt and pepper to taste

    Clean fish and wash well. If they are small leave whole. If it is a big fish cut into servings. Put in a big bowl, add salt, pour lemon juice over it and leave it for about an hour to be marinated. Heat oil in a frying pan. Add onions, carrots, celery, parsley and garlic. Add tomatoes, tomato purée, bay leaves, oregano, salt and pepper. Stir and lower heat. Let sauce cook for about 20—25 minutes. Put a layer of potatoes in a big pan and put fish over them. Add the sauce and cook in the oven (medium — 350ºF) for 50—60 minutes. Serve hot and put in each plate, pieces of fish, potatoes, vegetables and sauce.

Makes 6—8 dishes.

"KSIFIAS STA KARVOUNA" — SWORD FISH ON CHARCOAL

2 kilos sword fish
4 big tomatoes cut into 2 cm cubes
3 onions cut in the middle and
    separated in leaves
4 green peppers cut into big
    pieces
3 whole mushrooms for each spit
½ cup of parsley, finely chopped

½ cup of onions, finely chopped
½ cup of lemon juice
½ cup of olive oil
Salt and pepper to taste

Cut fish into 2 to 4 cm cubes. Put cubes in a big dish and season. Pour half of the lemon juice over it. Let it marinate for about an hour. In the meantime beat olive-oil with lemon juice. Pass fish on skewers alternately with mushrooms, tomatoes, onions or green pepper and so on. Cook on a very low heat, for about 20—30 minutes. Turn the skewers over, now and then, and brush the fish with the beaten oil and lemon juice. Serve hot. Pour the rest of the lemon juice and olive oil over it and sprinkle with onions and parsley.

For 5—7 persons.

"OCTAPODHI STIFADHO"* OCTOPUS WITH ONIONS

1 octopus about one kilo, well beaten
10 black pepper corns
4 cloves of garlic, finely chopped
2 bayleaves
1 large piece of cinnamon
1 cup of hot water
½ cup of olive oil
½ cup of wine vinegar
½ kilo of grated tomatoes
½ kilo of very small onions
    peeled but not cut
Salt to taste

Separate tentacles from octopus head. Remove eyes, beak and intestines and throw away. Wash octopus and tentacles well and put them in a pan. Heat the pan for 15 minutes until octopus juice is evaporated. Drain and when cool cut in small pieces. In a deep saucepan heat the oil and put garlic. Stir and add octopus. Fry octopus for 10 minutes and pour the vinegar. Stir for a while and add the grated tomatoes, pepper corns, bayleaves, salt and one cup of hot water. Reduce heat, cover the pan, and simmer for one hour. Then add the small onions and simmer the food for another hour, until octopus is tender. Serve hot.

Makes 6—8 dishes.

"SOUPIES YIAHNI" — CUTTLEFISH WITH ONIONS

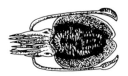

1 kilo of cuttle fish
1 kilo of onions cut into thin slices
1 cup of oil
2 bayleaves
2 cups of hot water
½ cup of parsley, finely chopped
½ cup of red dry wine
Salt and pepper

Clean cuttlefish as follows: Remove eyes with a knife, as well as the intestines and the cuttle bone. Keep the ink. Wash the tentacles and cut them into small pieces. Wash fish several times, drain and cut into strips. Put oil in a pan to heat, and put the onions in it. Add the fish and the chopped tentacles. Cook for about 15 minutes. Then add the wine, parsley, bayleaves, salt, pepper and the ink removed from the fish. Stir the fish. Finally add the water, lower the heat and let cook for about one hour, until there is a thick sauce left in the pan. Serve hot!

Makes 6—8 dishes.

"KALAMARIA YIEMISTA" — STUFFED SQUID

1 cup of hot water
1½ kilo of small sized squids
½ cup of olive oil

For stuffing:
4 tblsps of rice
2 cloves
1 cup of hot water
½ cup of cornoil
½ cup of onion, finely chopped

½ cup of white dry wine
½ cup of tomato purée
½ tsp of dry mint
½ tsp of cinnamon
Salt and pepper

Cut out and discard the eyes and the beak of the squid. Pul the head and tentacles apart from the body. Remove dark skin from the head and rinse well. Cut head and tentacles in very small pieces and put them in a sieve to drain. Remove the intestines, dark skin, and the backbone from inside. Rinse well and drain. In a small saucepan heat the oil and put squid bags to fry until golden, and put them aside. Then put onions to get soft and add tentacles to fry until all liquid is evaporated. Add the wine, stir, and pour the tomato purée dissolved in a cup of hot water, the cinnamon, mint, cloves salt and pepper. Reduce heat, cover the pan and simmer gently for 30 minutes. Wash rice, pour in saucepan and simmer for another 15 minutes until liquid is absorbed and the mixture is thick. With this mixture fill the squid, leaving some space for expansion. Sew the opening with strong thread and place them in rows in a small deep pan. Pour over them the olive oil and cup of hot water. Cover the pan and cook on low heat for one hour until squid are tender. Serve hot.

Makes about 7 dishes.

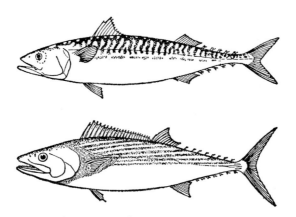

"PSARI PLAKI" — FISH WITH TOMATO SAUCE*

1½ kilo of fish (small or large)
3 cloves of garlic, finely chopped
1 cup of onions cut into rings
2 tblsps of parsley, finely chopped
1 cup of corn oil
1 tblsp of tomato purée
½ kilo of tomatoes, peeled
   and finely chopped
½ cup of dry white wine
¼ cup of lemon juice
Salt and pepper to taste

Clean and wash fish. If small, do not cut. If big, cut into individual portions. Put in bowl, sprinkle with a tblsp salt and the lemon juice. Let stand, for about an hour. Heat oil in a pan and put the garlic and the onion in it. Add wine and when it boils add the tomatoes, parsley, pepper and ½ cup of water. Cook on low heat for about 25 minutes. Remove the pan from the heat. Put the fish in a fireproof dish. Arrange the pieces evenly. Cover the fish with sauce. Dissolve the tomato purée in about ½ cup of warm water. Add this to the dish and shake lightly (to allow the tomato paste to cover the sauce evenly). Put the dish into the oven and bake at medium heat (300—350ºF) for about 30—35 minutes. When the "plaki" is ready the sauce will be nice and thick.

Makes about 6—8 dishes.

Note: The fish "plaki" can also be cooked in the stoneware in the same way as above.

53

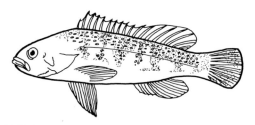

"PESTROFA TOU SPITIOU" — TROUT AS COOKED AT HOME*

6—8 big trout
2 kilos of potatoes cut into thin
  slices
1 cup of carrots cut into thin
  round slices
4 cloves of garlic
1 kilo of tomatoes, cut in thick
  slices
1 tblsp of tomato purée
2 bay leaves
1 tsp of oregano
2 cups of fresh milk
1 cup of vinegar
½ cup of lemon juice
½ cup of onions, finely chopped
½ cup of parsley, finely chopped
½ cup of celery, finely chopped
½ cup of olive oil
Salt and pepper

Clean the trout, drain, and put in a bowl with the milk. Let stand for about 30 minutes. Wash the trout first with water; then with a cup of vinegar. Put them again into a glass bowl. Add salt, pepper, and pour lemon juice over them. Let stand for another 30 minutes. In the meantime prepare the sauce. Put olive oil in a medium-sized pan and add onions and garlic. Add carrots, celery, parsley, stir and heat for 5 minutes. Dissolve the tomato purée in a cup of hot water and pour it into the frying pan together with salt, pepper bay leaves and oregano and cook for 15 more minutes. Put potatoes in a tray and cover them with the fish. Next put the thick slices of tomatoes on top of the trout. Put the tray on the stove fire for about 5 minutes and then put in the oven (350ºF) for 40—55 minutes. Serve the fish hot. Put one fish, some vegetables and sauce in each plate.

Makes 6—8 dishes.

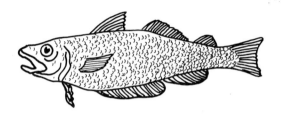

"BACALIAROS SCORDHALIA" — DRIED COD
WITH GARLIC SAUCE*

1 kilo of dried cod
1 medium onion, cut in half
2 carrots cleaned, cut in half
2 celery stalks cut in half
6 cloves of garlic
2 cups of mashed potatoes
1 cup of olive oil
¼ cup of wine vinegar
¼ cup of parsley, finely chopped

Put the dried cod in cold water for about 3 hours. Meanwhile, change the water 2—3 times. Remove its skin and cut into big pieces. Then put cod in a pan of cold water; add the onion, carrots and celery and boil for one hour. Put in a platter and remove its bones. Cut in smaller pieces.

Now prepare the "scordalia" (garlic sauce). Pound the garlic until it becomes creamy. Put in a bowl. Gradually add the mashed potatoes and stir. Add alternately oil and vinegar, until it becomes a smooth cream. Sprinkle with parsley. Serve cod hot or cold, with this garlic sauce.

Makes 5—7 dishes.

55

"KIMATHES" — MINCED MEAT

"MELINTZANES YIEMISTES" — STUFFED EGG PLANTS

1½ kilo of medium size eggplants

For the stuffing:
3 eggs
2 medium size onions, finely chopped
¾ kilo of minced meat, pork and beef
½ cup of white dry wine
½ cup of breadcrumbs
½ kilo of peeled tomatoes, finely chopped
½ cup of grated cheese
½ cup of corn oil
Salt and pepper

For the cream:
3 cups of fresh milk
3 egg yolks
4 tblsps of corn oil
4 tblsps of flour
½ cup of grated cheese
¼ tsp of nutmeg
Salt and pepper

Wash eggplants and cut them in half lengthwise. With a teaspoon scoop out each half eggplant leaving a thick wall, and making them look like little boats. Keep half the quantity of eggplant's flesh. Fry eggplants in hot oil until they get light brown. Place them in rows in a baking-tray. Then prepare the stuffing: In a small saucepan heat half of the used oil and put the onion to get soft. Add minced meat, stir and cook to get light brown. Then pour the wine, stir, and add the eggplants flesh, tomatoes, salt and pepper. Stir again and simmer for 30 minutes. Remove saucepan from heat and add breadcrumbs and eggs. Mix well and cover saucepan. Now prepare the cream: Bring milk to boil, set aside and keep hot. Heat oil in a pan and gradually pour flour stirring at the same time until it becomes a thick paste. Then add the milk and stir until paste becomes a smooth cream. Remove pan from the heat, add egg yolks, cheese, nutmeg, salt, pepper and mix thoroughly. Finally place stuffing in eggplants, but don't fill completely. Keep a small space, and fill it up with cream. Sprinkle some grated cheese on the cream. Place eggplants in oven and bake on medium oven for 30 minutes, until golden.

Makes 8—10 dishes.

"MOUSAKKAS" — SLICED VEGETABLES WITH LAYERS OF SPICED MINCED MEAT

Vegetables
1 kilo potatoes
1 cup of grated cheese
½ kilo eggplants
½ kilo marrows, zucchini

For the cream
3 cups of milk
4 tblsps of oil
4 tblsps of flour
4 egg yolks
1 cup of grated cheese
¼ tsp nutmeg
Salt and pepper

For the minced meat sauce
1 tblsp of onion, thinly chopped
1 kilo of minced meat
2 tblsps of parsley, thinly chopped
1 cup of ripe tomatoes, thinly chopped
1 tsp of tomato purée
½ cup of corn oil
½ cup of dry white wine
Salt and pepper

Preparation of the meat sauce

Heat oil in a frying pan and add onions to get soft. Add meat and stir until it is light brown. Add wine and let it boil for two minutes. Then add the parsley, the chopped tomatoes and the tomato purée, dissolved in one cup of hot water. Lower heat and cook for 30 minutes. Add salt and pepper.

Preparation of the cream

Heat oil in a small pan and gradually add flour, stirring at the same time to become a thick cream. Add milk (quite hot) little by little and keep on stirring. When it is quite thick remove pan from heat and mix with the egg yolks, the grated cheese, the nutmeg, salt and pepper.

Final preparation for mousakkas

Peel the potatoes, eggplants and marrows and cut them into thick long slices. Put oil in the pan until it is very hot and fry the above vegetables until they are light brown. Grease a pan and line the bottom with one layer of potatoes. Sprinkle with cheese and nutmeg. Add a layer of eggplants, some cheese and finally a layer of marrows. Cover the marrows with a thick meat sauce and repeat with alternative layers of marrows potatoes and eggplants. Cover the contents of the pan with the cream. Sprinkle with grated cheese and put in medium oven until light brown. Cool and cut into square serving pieces. It is served hot as well as cold; it can be served as an appetizer as well as a main dish.

Makes about 10 dishes.

"KOUPEPIA" — STUFFED VINE LEAVES

60—70 fresh or tinned vine leaves
2 tblsps of finely chopped parsley
2 tblsps of finely chopped onions
1 tblsp of finely chopped mint or
  ½ tblsp dry mint
1 cup of ripe, peeled tomatoes,
  finely chopped
1 kilo of ground meat (pork and
  veal mixed)
½ cup of rice
The white of 2 eggs
Salt and pepper
The juice of one lemon
Meat broth or water as desired

For the sauce:

2 tblsps of flour
2 tblsps of butter
2 egg yolks
2 cups of hot meat broth
The juice of two lemons

Wash the wine leaves and put them into boiling salted water for 3—4 minutes so that they become soft. Then dip them in cold water and set aside. Put the ground meat, the chopped onions, mint, parsley, salt, pepper and the whites of the eggs into a bowl. Wash the rice and put it in lukewarm water for approximately 5 minutes. Drain the rice and mix well with the lemon juice. Add the rice to the meat mixture and knead well. Open the vine leaves one by one and put 1 tsp of the prepared meat mixture near the edge of the leaf. Wrap it well, starting with the part where the mixture is and rolling the leaf as you would roll coins, remembering to fold the ends so the mixture does not fall out. Put the stuffed vine leaves in rows in a pan. Cover with a heavy soup plate and add enough broth or water just to cover them. Simmer for 40 minutes. Now prepare the sauce: Beat the egg yolks with the lemon juice. In a small saucepan melt the butter and gradually add the flour stirring at the same time until it becomes a thick cream. Remove saucepan from the heat, add the meat broth and stir until mixture is a smooth thinly sauce. Pour in the sauce the egg mixture, stir and heat for another 3 minutes. When "koupepia" are cooked pour the sauce over them and serve hot.

Makes 10 dishes.

Note: If there are no vine leaves, cabbage leaves can be used instead.

"DHIAFORA PARAYIEMISTA" — VARIOUS STUFFED VEGETABLES

4 ripe round tomatoes
4 medium sized green peppers
4 medium sized zucchini
4 outer shells of big onions
½ cup of corn oil

For stuffing:
1 large onion, finely chopped
1 tblsp of parsley, finely chopped
2 tblsps of lemon juice
½ kilo of minced beef and pork
½ cup of rice

½ cup of finely chopped tomatoes
¼ tsp of cinnamon powder
Salt and pepper

For sause:
The pulp from tomatoes
1 medium size onion, finely chopped
1 tblsp of tomato purée
1 cup of hot meat broth
1 bay leaf
½ tsp of sugar
Salt and pepper

Wash vegetables. Cut tops of tomatoes and peppers and keep in a plate. With a teaspoon scoop out zucchinis flesh. Repeat the same for tomatoes but save the pulp. Cut the two ends of onions and remove the hard outer layers. Drop them in boiling water for 2—3 minutes to get soft and remove the first two soft outer layers from each onion. Empty the inside membranes and seeds from peppers. Heat oil in a deep pan and put zucchini and peppers until light brown. Remove from pan and drain. Pour in the same pan the chopped onion until soft, add the pulp of tomatoe and stir. Dissolve tomato purée in a cup of hot meat broth and pour in the pan.

Add sugar, salt, pepper and bayleaf. Gently simmer the sauce for 15 minutes and remove from heat. Now prepare the stuffing: In a bowl put the minced meat and add onion, parsley, tomatoes, cinnamon, salt and pepper. Wash rice in lukewarm water and drain. Pour the lemon juice in the rice mixing well and add it to the minced meat. Knead mixture for 5 minutes to mix well. Place stuffing in vegetables leaving a space for expansion, and replace on each vegetable the small tops. Arrange stuffed vegetables upright in the pan next to each other. Cover vegetables with the tomato sauce. Add more water if necessary. Place a heavy soup plate on vegetables. Cover the pan and bring to the boil. Reduce heat and simmer gently for one hour. Place a variety of stuffed vegetables in every plate and cover them with thick sauce from the pan. Serve hot.

Makes 6—8 dishes.

"ROLO" — MINCED MEAT LOAF

1 kilo of minced lamb
4 hard-boiled eggs
3 fresh eggs
2 tblsps of finely chopped onions
2 tblsps of finely chopped parsley
2 tblsps of bread crumbs
1 cup of finely chopped tomatoes
1 lamb suet (approx. 10 sq. inches)
1 cube of chicken broth
1 cup of hot water
½ tsp of origano
¼ kilo of minced pork
Salt and pepper to taste

In a big bowl beat the eggs and mix salt, pepper and origano. Add minced meat, onions, parsley, bread crumbs and tomatoes. Knead mixture for 5 minutes to blend well. Spread the lamb suet. Place in the center the minced meat mixture and form a long and narrow shape 9X5 inches. Make a groove in the middle of minced mixture. Shell the boiled eggs and put them lengthwise in the groove. Cover the eggs with the minced mixture and roll in the suet. Put meat loaf in a fireproof dish. Dissolve broth cube in a cup of hot water and pour over the meat loaf. Cover the dish with aluminium foil. Bake in medium oven for one hour. After 45 minutes, remove the foil, thus allowing the meat loaf to get golden. When it is almost cold cut it in thin slices. Serve hot or cold.

Makes 6—8 dishes.

"KEFTEDHES ARNISIOUS SKHARAS" — LAMB PATTIES "CYPRIOT STYLE"

1 kilo New Zealand lamb, minced
1 small onion, grated
1 teaspoon salt
1 cup of pine nuts or blanched almonds
  roughly chopped
½ teaspoon black pepper
½ teaspoon grated nutmeg

Preheat the grill to high.

In a large bowl, combine all the ingredients together, mixing well until the mixture is well blended. Form into 12 small patties. Place the lamb patties on a rack in the grill pan and place them under the heat. Cook them for 8 minutes on each side or until the patties are cooked through. It the patties brown too quickly, reduce the heat to moderate after the first 2 minutes. Serve immediately with toast and a green salad.

4 servings.

"ANGINARES YEMISTES" — STUFFED ARTICHOKES

12 fresh or tinned whole artichokes
1 tblsp of salt
½ cup of flour
½ cup of lemon juice

For stuffing
1 tblsp of finely choped onion
1 tblsp of finely chopped parsley
1 cup of finely chopped tomatoes
½ cup of dry white wine
½ kilo of ground meat
¼ cup of oil
Salt and pepper

For cream:
3 tblsps of flour
3 tblsps of butter
4 cups of fresh milk
3 egg yolks
2 tblsps of grated cheese
¼ tsp of nutmeg
Salt and pepper

Peel off the hard outer leaves of the artichokes (if fresh) and one by one put the cleaned artichokes in water with flour, salt and lemon juice. Wash them and boil them in salted water; then drain. Heat the oil in a saucepan and fry the onions. Add the ground meat, parsley, and simmer until the water evaporates. Add wine and let it boil. Then add the tomatoes, salt and pepper and simmer for about 20 minutes. Now prepare the cream. Heat the butter in a pan and gradually add the flour while stirring until it becomes a thick sauce. In the meantime boil milk and add it; stirr again. Remove the pan from the stove and add the grated cheese, egg yolks, nutmeg, salt and pepper stirring at the same time. Finally, halfstuff the artichokes and fill them up with the cream. On top sprinkle some grated cheese. Bake in the oven (medium) for 30 minutes or until they become light golden brown.

Makes 6—8 dishes.

61

"LACHAM - ATZEEN" —
SPICED MINCED LAMB ON FLAT BREAD*

Although Lacham-atzeen is a Middle-East food, it is well-liked and very popular in Cyprus.

For minced meat mixtures:

3 cloves of garlic
1 large onion, finely chopped
1 cup of ripe, chopped tomatoes
1 tsp of chili red pepper, finely chopped
½ kilo of minced lamb
½ cup of finely chopped parsley
½ cup of corn oil
Salt and pepper

For the dough:

4 cup of hard flour
1 tsp of salt
1 tblsp of dried yeast
1 tblsp of oil
1½ cup of lukewarm water

Sift flour and keep half of it aside. Dissolve the yeast in water and add salt. Pour half of the flour into the yeast mixture and stir until thick. Cover with a thick towel and leave until frothy. Then mix the rest of the flour and knead gradually adding the oil, until it becomes smooth and elastic. Form it into a ball, put it in a bowl, cover top with a thick towel and leave it for one hour until it rises. Then knead again for another five minutes, divide into 20 equal portions and shape each one into a ball. Roll each ball to 4 inches in diameter and ¼ of inch in thickness and place them on a greased baking tray. Spread on each piece of dough 2—3 tablespoons of mince mixture and put in hot oven for 30 minutes. You can serve "Lacham-Atzeen" hot or cold. Sprinkle lemon juice on top.

Makes 20 pieces.

"POULERICA" — POULTRY

It is common in Cyprus for families to keep chickens. This is not restricted only to villages. If a special occasion arises, such as the sudden arrival of friends or relatives, the visit of a foreigner or the late return of the family from the church, a chicken can be slaughtered. The hostess takes great care of her chicken-coop for it is an invaluable source of delicious meals. In a short time a smart hostess can prepare a good hot dish of chicken ready for her guests. The meal almost invariably includes a good portion of macaroni cooked in the broth.

The preparation of such a meal is very simple yet yields a nourishing and tasty dish.

63

"KOTOPOULO VRASTO ME MAKARONIA" BOILED CHICKEN AND MACARONI

1 chicken weighing 1½—2 kilos
1½ cup of halloumi (Cyprus cheese)
   or any other kind of grated cheese
1 tblsp of salt
½ kilo of thick macaroni

Clean the chicken and wash well. Put it whole, in a pot full of salted water, and cook for about an hour. We shall know when it is cooked, when the meat of the wings start to separate from the bones. Put chicken on a platter, cut into pieces and put 3—4 quarters of lemon round the chicken. Pour the macaroni to the hot broth and cook on medium heat for about 15 minutes. Put macaroni in a big soup plate together with some of the broth and sprinkle with a lot of grated cheese. Serve macaroni and chicken hot.

Makes 6—8 dishes.

"FRANGOLINA STO FOURNO" — OVEN BAKED GUINEA-FOWL

1 guinea-fowl
1 tblsp salt
1 cup of guinea-hen broth
2 bayleaves
½ cup of fresh butter
½ cup of lemon juice

Pluck the feathers of the guinea-fowl and singe it over alcohol flame. Remove the intestines and cut the liver and stomach into small pieces. Wash the bird in cold water. In a saucepan put the guinea-fowl, add some water and salt and boil for about 45 minutes. Remove the guinea-fowl from the saucepan and put it in a strainer. Place the bayleaves inside the bird and put it in a tray. Spread the butter over the bird, put the tray in a medium heat oven and bake for about 45—55 minutes. Remove the tray from the oven and place the guinea-fowl on a platter. Put the liver and stomach pieces in the tray and heat them on low fire for about 10 minutes. Pour the lemon juice, stir for a while and when the lemon juice begins to evaporate add a cup of guinea-fowl broth. Leave for about 10 minutes to boil and when the sauce thickens pour it into a small saucepan. Place the saucepan on low heat to keep it hot, until the food is served. Cut the bird into pieces and pour its sauce over it. Accompany it with potatoes cooked in the oven, rice pilaff, or ground wheat cooked in the guineafowl broth.

Makes 8—10 dishes.

"KOTOPOULO KAOURMAS" — CASSEROLE CHICKEN WITH POTATOES

1 cup of dry white wine
1½ kilo of potatoes
10—12 small, whole onions
1 chicken weighing 1 kilo
1 cup of corn oil
1 cup of hot water
Salt and pepper

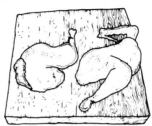

Clean the chicken, wash and drain. Peel potatoes, wash and cut into quarters. Clean the onions, wash and drain. Fry onions first then the potatoes and put them in a bowl. In a saucepan fry the chicken until light brown. Add wine, and when it boils, add salt, pepper and water. Cover the pan, lower the heat and simmer for about an hour. Twenty minutes before the pan is removed from heat, put onions in it and the potatoes so that they are ready together with the chicken. Serve chicken hot and put some onions and potatoes in each plate. Pour sauce left in the sauce pan, over them.

Makes 4—6 dishes.

"KOTOPOULO LEMONATO" CHICKEN COOKED IN LEMON SAUCE

1 chicken weighing 1—1½ kilo
1 kilo of small spring potatoes
2 cups of corn oil
½ cup of lemon juice
Hot water (as much as needed)
Salt and pepper

Clean the chicken, wash and cut in 8 pieces. In a pan put half of the oil and when hot put the chicken in it until it becomes light brown. Then add lemon juice salt and pepper. When it is very hot, add some hot water, just to cover the chicken. Lower the heat, cover pan, and simmer for about 60—75 minutes, until the sauce thickens.

In the meantime, choose small round potatoes. Peel them, wash and drain. Put the rest of the oil in a frying pan to heat and add the potatoes. When they become light brown, cover the pan and lower heat for 10 minutes until they soften. Serve chicken hot, put potatoes beside it and pour sauce over them.

Makes 6—8 dishes.

"KOTOPOULO ELENIS" — CHICKEN A LA ELENI

1½ kilo of artichokes, cleaned, whole
1 chicken (about a kilo)
2 tblsps of fresh dill or 1 tblsp dry dill
1 tblsp of tomato purée
2 cups of hot water
½ cup of corn oil
½ kilo of ripe, peeled tomatoes
Salt and pepper

Clean the chicken, wash and cut into 4 pieces. Cut tomatoes in small pieces. Heat oil in a saucepan and add the chicken until it is light brown. Remove the chicken. Repeat with artichokes. If you use fresh dill, put it in the oil. If not, put in the food, when the salt and pepper are added. Then put the cut tomatoes and the tomato purée (dissolved in ½ cup of lukewarm water), in the saucepan. Heat the sauce for about 5—6 minutes, add the remaining hot water, stir, and add the artichokes and the chicken. Add salt and pepper, lower heat and simmer in covered saucepan for about 45 minutes, or until the sauce is quite thick. Serve chicken hot, with the sauce. It is accompanied by a plain rice pilaff.

Makes 4—6 dishes.

"PERISTERIA ME PIZELI" — PIGEONS WITH PEAS*

3 small young pigeons
6—10 small onions, whole
1 kilo of peas
3 cloves of garlic, finely chopped
1 cup of hot water
½ cup of butter
½ cup of dry white wine
Salt and pepper

Peel onions, cutting only the "head" so that they stay whole. Remove feathers from the pigeons and pass the birds over the flame just to get slightly burnt on the outside and to clean completely from feathers. Remove intestines, wash and cut the birds into pieces. Fry onions and garlic and put in a platter. Put the pigeons in the frying pan until they are light brown. Add wine. When it is hot add salt, pepper and water and simmer for about an hour. Twenty minutes before the pan is removed from the heat, add the onions and the peas (after they are well-drained) so that they are cooked together with the pigeons. Serve hot putting in each plate half a pigeon, 1—2 onions, peas and sauce.

Makes 6 dishes.

"KHINOPOULO PARAYEMISTO" — STUFFED GOOSE

1 Goose weighing about 2 kilos
1 cup of rice
1 cup of butter
1 cup of dry white wine
1 cup of hot water
1 cup of chestnuts boiled peeled and cut
  into medium size pieces
1 cup of apples cut into thick slices
½ kilo of minced beef meat
½ cup of finely chopped onion
Salt and pepper

Pluck the feathers of the goose, singe it over alcohol flame and dry it with a serviette. Remove the intestines, wash the goose well and leave it in a cool place for a day to drain.

The following day, prepare the stuffing. Put half of the butter in a wide frying pan to heat and sauté the onion. Add the minced meat, salt, pepper, rice, apples and chestnuts. Leave them to heat for about 5—6 minutes, add the wine and stir for a while. Finally add the water, lower the heat and cook the stuffing slowly until all the water is absorbed. In the meantime turn on the oven so that it gets warm.

Mix the salt and pepper and sprinkle it inside the goose. Leave the stuffing to cool and fill the inside part of the goose with it. Sew the slit and using a special string tie up the legs to the tail, and the wings to the body.

Place a grill into a pan and put the goose on it with its back on the grill. Spread the rest of the butter over the goose and roll it in aluminum foil. Be careful, however, to roll it in such a way that the aluminum foil does not touch the goose because if it does the heat will burn it. In other words, there must be some place left between the bird and the aluminum foil. Then, put the pan in the oven and cook the goose slowly with a low heat of 350⁰F for about 3 hours. Do not open the oven while it is being cooked.

After the goose has been in the oven for two hours, only then can you open the oven and check whether it is cooked or not.

You can find out if the bird is cooked or not by pressing its leg with your fingers. If, when you do that the leg is soft, then the bird is cooked. You can also move its leg, and if the movement is easy and light, this means that the goose is cooked.

Makes 10—15 dishes.

"GALOPOULO KATSAROLLAS" — CASSEROLE TURKEY*

1 turkey weighing about 2 kilos
1 cup of dry white wine
1 tblsp of flour
2 cups of ripe tomatoes, finely cut
1 cup of hot water
1 bayleaf
2 cloves of garlic, finely cut
½ cup of butter
½ cup of finely chopped onion
Salt and pepper

Wash the turkey well and drain it. Cut it into ordinary portions (two pieces for each person).

Put the butter in a saucepan to melt, and fry the turkey until it is light brown on all sides. Then sauté onion and garlic. Sprinkle over them the flour, salt and pepper. Stir for 2 minutes and add the wine. When it starts boiling add the tomatoes, water and bayleaf. Lower the heat, cover the saucepan and cook slowly for about 2 hours.

While it is being cooked add some more hot water if necessary. When it is cooked the sause must be rather thick. Serve it hot together with its sauce and accompany it with rice pilaff.

Please look at page 44 for the recipe of rice pilaff.

Makes 10—15 dishes.

"KINIGI" — GAME

"TSIKLES ME SALTSA KRASIOU" — THRUSH IN WINE SAUCE

6 thrushes
1 cup of butter
3 slices of bacon, finely cut
6 black olives stoned and finely cut
1 cup of dry white wine
2 cups of hot water
½ cup of mushrooms cut into thin slices
Salt and pepper

Pluck the feathers of the thrushes and singe them. Remove their intestines and cut their liver into small pieces. Cut their beaks, the ends of their wings and their feet. Using a pair of scissors cut the bird across the back and press it slightly to open up. Wash, drain them and sprinkle them with salt and pepper.

In a wide saucepan heat the butter, fry the birds until they are light brown and then put them on a platter. Sauté liver, and repeat the same for mushrooms, olives and bacon.

Put the fried birds back into the saucepan to heat and add the wine. Stir for 5 minutes and add the hot water. Lower the heat to medium, cover the saucepan and cook slowly for about an hour.

In the meantime, watch them at intervals while they are being cooked and when necessary add a cup of hot water. When the food is cooked, the sauce must be rather thick.

Serve them hot on fried bread, and pour their sauce over them.

Makes 6 dishes.

"ORTIKIA SKHARAS" — GRILLED QUAILS

2 quails
½ cup of lemon juice
½ cup of oil
½ cup of bread crumbs
Salt and pepper

First, light the charcoal. Pluck the feathers of the quails and singe them. Remove their intestines and wash the quails well. Drain them, and using a special pair of scissors cut them across their backs. Press them slightly to open up and sprinkle them with salt and pepper. Mix the oil and the lemon juice in a bowl and beat them well. Dip the quails into the mixture of oil and lemon juice and then dip them into the bread crumbs. Put them on the grill and cook them over the charcoal with low heat for about one hour. I would like to stress that they must be cooked on very low heat because during cooking the charcoal flames up and can blacken them.

Makes 2 dishes.

"LAGOS STO FOURNO" — OVEN-BAKED WILD RABBIT

Ingredients for the marinate

2 small carrots, thickly cut
3 stalks of celery, thickly chopped
10 sprigs of parsley, thickly chopped
1 big onion, thickly chopped
2 small ripe tomatoes cut in the shape
   of a cross
A mixture of 1 cup of dry red wine,
   1 cup of vinegar and
   3 cups of water, to cover the rabbit

Ingredients for the cooking

1 rabbit weighing 1½—2 kilos
2 cups of onion cut into thick slices
1 cup of ripe tomatoes, finely cut
2 cloves of garlic, finely cut
3 slices of bacon, finely cut
2 bayleaves
1 cinnamon stick
1 cup of vegetable oil
1 cup of hot water
1 cup of dry white wine
1 tsp of salt
½ cup of flour
½ tsp of pepper

Before I start explaining the way to cook the rabbit, I would like to stress that, because the meat of wild, hunted animals is harder and has a stronger smell than the meat of other animals, a special preparation and a good marinate are necessary before cooking them. In the case of a wild rabbit, after removing its skin and intestines, put it in the refrigerator and leave it for about two days to drain.

Then cut the animal as follows: Cut its front and back legs. Cut its two sides, the neck and its back into 4 pieces. Then cut these big pieces into smaller ones. The marinading procedure follows. In a clay pot or glass bowl put the rabbit pieces and the vegetables of the marinate. Pour the wine mixture over them, and cover them with a big plate so that they stay under the wine mixture. Leave the rabbit to marinate for about 8—10 hours.

Remove the meat and put it in a strainer to drain completely and then cook it in the following way. First of all, turn on the oven to get warm. Dip the rabbit pieces in flour and then pat them so that most of the flour falls off.

Pour the oil into a wide frying pan to heat and fry the rabbit pieces until they are light brown. Then, put them into a clay pot or into a pie-dish.

Using the same frying pan, sauté the bacon and garlic and then sauté the onion. Add the wine, stir for a while until boiling, add the tomatoes, water, salt and pepper, cinnamon stick and bayleaves. Stir again, for a while, lower the heat and cook slowly for about 10 minutes. Empty the contents of the frying pan into the clay pot or pie-dish with the fried rabbit pieces and place it in the oven at a medium temperature of 350°F for about 90—100 minutes.

Makes 10—12 dishes.

"BEKATSES ME SALTSA TOMATA" — WOODCOCK IN TOMATO SAUCE

2 woodcocks
1 cup of dry white wine
2 cups of grated ripe tomatoes
½ cup of butter
¼ cup of finely cut onion
¼ cup of parsley, finely cut
1 cup of hot water

Pluck the feathers of the woodcocks and singe them over alcohol flame.

Remove the intestines and cut the liver into small pieces. Wash the woodcocks and cut them lengthwise into halves. Dry them and sprinkle them with salt and pepper. Put the butter in a saucepan to heat and fry the birds until they are light brown on all sides. Sauté the liver, and then sauté the onion and parsley. Add the wine to boil and then add the tomatoes and water. Lower the heat, cover the saucepan and cook the woodcocks slowly for about 1½ hour.

Makes 4 dishes.

"PAPIA KATSAROLAS" — DUCK CASSEROLE

1 duck weighing 1½—2 kilos
1 cup of vegetable oil
1 cup of butter
2 bayleaves
2—3 cups of hot water
½ cup of finely cut parsley
½ cup of lemon juice
Salt and pepper

Pluck the feathers of the duck and singe it over alcohol flame. Remove the intestines and wash the duck. Leave it to drain, dry it with a piece of cloth and spread the oil all over it. Leave it in a cool place for about 1—2 hour so that its skin softens. Then, cut it into 6—8 pieces.

Put the butter in a saucepan to melt and fry the duck pieces until they are light brown on all sides. Add the lemon juice and stir until it evaporates and until the bottom of the saucepan gets a dark colour. Add the three cups of hot water, the parley, salt, pepper and bayleaves.

Lower the heat, cover the saucepan and cook slowly for about 1½—2 hours depending on the age of the bird. Watch it at intervals while it is being cooked and when there is only a little water left, add some more so that when the food is cooked the sauce is rather thick.

Serve the duck hot and accompany it with mashed potatoes and various boiled vegetables, sauté in butter and with the duck sauce poured over them.

Makes 6—8 dishes.

"PERDHIKES STO FOURNO" — OVEN-BAKED PARTRIDGES

2 partridges
2 thick slices of halloumi or any
 other kind of hard cheese
2 thick slices of a ripe tomato
6 slices of bacon
1 cup of butter
½ cup of lemon juice
Salt and pepper

Pluck the feathers of the partridges and singe them. Remove their intestines, wash them well, drain them and keep them in the refrigerator for 2—3 days. Then, coat the skin of the partridges with lemon juice, and sprinkle them with salt and pepper inside and outside. Put a slice of halloumi and a slice of tomato inside the bird. Using a special needle sew up the slit. Put three slices of bacon around each partridge and fasten them with a toothpick. Place the partridges in a small pan, add the butter and the rest of the lemon juice and cover them with aluminium foil. Put the pan in the oven and cook at 325ºF for about 1—2 hours depending on the age of the bird. Twenty minutes before removing the pan from the oven, remove the aluminium foil so that the partridges get a light brown colour.

Makes 4 dishes.

Note: The right time for cooking the partridges will be decided by discovering the age of the bird which can be found by examining its legs. If on the lower part of its leg there is no distinctive knot, this means that the bird is less than a year old and it needs about an hour to be cooked. If there is a small knot the bird is more than a year old and it needs about 1½ hour to be cooked. Finally, if the knot is big, the bird needs about 2 hours to be cooked.

"ARNI" — LAMB

"ARNI TTAVAS" — OVEN-ROAST LAMB AND ONIONS

"Ttavas" is popular and well-liked by all Cypriots. Actually it is made in a clay pot called "ttavas" or "ntavas". It looks like a deep soup bowl, without a cover. The food is always cooked without a cover, even if it is cooked in a glass fire proof or a copper pot. When I used to work in a small restaurant, in 1944, in Limassol, my manager used to cook "ttavas" in small individual clay pots, and after they were cooked, he kept them hot on low charcoals.

1 kilo of lamb shoulder
1 kilo of onions, cut into thin
  slices
1 kilo or ripe tomatoes, finely
  chopped
1 tsp of cumin seed
2 small pieces of cinnamon
1 cup of lukewarm water
¼ cup of winevinegar
½ cup of corn oil
Salt and pepper

Cut lamb in 20—25 pieces. Heat oil in a frying pan and put lamb in it. Fry until light brown. Then put lamb into a "ttava" pot or any other pot. Fry onions and put oil and onions into the meat. Add winevinegar, half of the cumin seed, cinnamon, salt, pepper and tomatoes. Mix well, and put "ttavas" in the oven in a medium heat, for about 2 hours.

Stir every 30 minutes. Serve quite hot and sprinkle some of the cumin seed in each plate. Accompany it with a simple pilaff "pourgouri" or any other kind of pilaff, and with yoghurt.

Makes 8—10 dishes.

"BOUTI ARNIOU ROSTO" — ROAST LEG OF LAMB*

2½ kilos leg of lamb
1 garlic clove, crushed
1 teaspoon grated lemon rind
1 teaspoon salt
freshly ground black pepper
2 tablespoons butter
2 tablespoons oil
2 tablespoons lemon juice
2 chopped onions
2 tablespoons chopped parsley
1 cup mushrooms, sliced

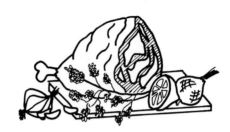

Preheat the oven to very hot 475⁰F (Gas Mark 9).

In a mixing bowl, put the garlic, lemon rind, salt and 6 grindings of black pepper. Mix well and spread over the lamb. Place the meat, skin side up into a roasting tin. In a small saucepan melt the butter and oil over low heat. Add the lemon juice and the stock, or water. Bring to the boil and pour into the roasting tin. Cook in the oven for 20 minutes. Reduce the heat to moderate 350⁰F (Gas Mark 4). Add onions, parsley, and mushrooms and cook for a further 2 hours. Place the meat on a serving dish and arrange the onion mixture around it with rice sauté in butter.

6 Servings.

"ARNI ENTRADHA" — LAMB BLANQUETTE

1 kilo breast and neck of lamb
2 sticks celery
1 bayleaf
½ kilo potatoes
½ cup of lemon juice
¼ kilo button onions
¼ kilo carrots
flour
salt
white pepper

Cut the meat into 2´´ pieces and bring to the boil in salted water. Refresh under cold water after the blanching. Fry gently adding plenty of flour to dry off, making sure that the flour is cooked but does not colour. Add carrots, button onions, salt, pepper, bayleaf, celery, lemon juice and simmer until cooked. Potatoes are added later. When cooked, the meat should easily separate from the bone.

4—6 servings.

"ARNI KAPPAMAS" —
LAMB AND POTATOES COOKED IN TOMATO SAUCE

1½ kilos of lamb shoulder cut in
   10—14 pieces
1 kilo of small round potatoes
1 tblsp of tomato purée
2 tblsp of flour
2 bayleaves
½ cup of corn oil
½ kilo of tomatoes
½ cup of dry white wine
½ cup of onion, finely chopped
¼ tsp of thyme
Salt and pepper

Peel wash and drain, potatoes. Pierce them with a knife. Sprinkle meat with flour and take away the excess flour. Fry potatoes in a saucepan and put them in a sieve. Heat onions to become soft and add the meat to fry until it is light brown. Then add the wine and when it is boiling add tomatoes, bayleaves, thyme, salt, pepper and the tomato purée dissolved in a cup of hot water. Heat for 10 minutes and add some more hot water just to cover the meat. Cover saucepan and cook on low heat for about one hour. 15 minutes before the saucepan is removed from the heat add the potatoes to cook with the lamb. Serve "Cappamas" hot with its sauce accompanied with various fresh vegetables cut in big pieces.

Makes 6—8 dishes.

Note: Although this is the original recipe, there are people, who make "Cappamas" without potatoes but they accompany it with macaroni or rice pilaff covered with the "cappama's" sauce.

"ARNI PSITO" — OVEN BAKED LAMB

Many Cypriot housewives cook this food only on Sundays, and the rest of the family look forward to this delicious dish. It is cooked either in the small oven, which is in the yard, or in the big oven where they bake the bread. It is also good, however, cooked in the kitchen's oven, for those who do not have either of the two alternatives.

>   1 leg of lamb weighing about 2 kilos
>   1 kilo of large potatoes
>   ½ cup of corn oil
>   ½ cup of cooking fat
>   ¼ cup of lemon juice
>   ½ kilo of ripe tomatoes, cut into
>   big slices
>   ½ cup of cold water
>   Salt and pepper

Peel potatoes, wash, cut them in quarters and put in a pie-dish. Wash lamb, drain, pour over it lemon juice and put it among the potatoes. Add the corn oil and the fat and sprinkle with salt and pepper. Lay cut tomatoes on the lamb and cook in the oven (medium) for about 1½—2 hours. Cut the leg in thin slices and accompany them with potatoes. A salad of various vegetables goes very well with the "Psito".

Makes 6—8 dishes.

"ARNI ME COUNOUPPIDHI MESARITICO" —
LAMB WITH CAULIFLOWER A LA MESAORIAS

1½ kilos of cauliflower
1 kilo of lamb breast
1 cup of finely chopped onions
1 cup of corn oil
1½ cups of red dry wine
Salt and pepper.

Cut lamb in medium pieces and put in a bowl. Tear the cauliflower starting at the bottom so that each part will contain both flower and stalk; put it in the bowl with meat. Pour wine over them and leave for 1—2 hours. Drain the cauliflower. Heat the oil in a casserole, and fry onions lightly. Fry cauliflower and put in a pie-dish. Fry the lamb and add the marinate-wine. When boiling, add a cup of hot water, salt and pepper, lower heat so that the lamb simmers in the covered pan for about 1½ hour. 30 minutes before the pan is removed from heat add cauliflower; put it among the meat so that its flowers face upwards. Add half a cup of water and the cauliflower will be cooked at the same time as the meat. Serve hot with vegetables cut in thick slices, in a separate plate.

Makes 6—8 dishes.

"KLEFTIKO" BAKED LAMB WRAPPED IN PAPER

"Kleftiko" is made of lamb or goat meat (not too young) and must be cooked in a sealed pot. In Cyprus, "kleftiko" is put in special pots made of clay and is cooked in small ovens which exist in almost every backyard. In the towns where there are no such special ovens, the housewives put the meat in a clay pot, seal it with paste made of flour and water and cook it in the usual kitchen oven. In a house where there is no pot made of clay, the housewife can use a pie-dish but this also should be sealed, so that the meat can be cooked very slowly. (When properly done the bone should separate from the meat very easily).

For those without the aid of an outdoor oven, cook as follows:

6 pieces of boned meat (¼ kilo approximately for every person)
3 big tomatoes cut in thick slices
2 tblsps of corn oil
1 kilo of small spring potatoes
6 small cubes of fat from lamb's tail
2 bayleaves cut in halves

1 tsp of salt
¼ tsp of pepper
¼ tblsp of oregano
¼ tblsp of thyme
¼ cup of lemon juice
½ cup of corn oil (for potatoes)
Salt and pepper

Wash the cut meat, drain well, sprinkle with lemon juice. Mix salt, pepper, oregano, thyme and sprinkle on the meat. Brush corn oil onto 6 big pieces of foil and wrap the meat in them. Put in the pot, seal well with paste and cook in medium oven for 2½ hours. Meanwhile prepare the potatoes. Peel them, wash them and make small cuts in each potato with a knife. Put in the baking tray. Add oil and lamb's fat. Put the sliced tomatoes on the potatoes; sprinkle with salt and pepper and add bayleaves. One hour before the lamb is ready, put potatoes in the oven too, so that they will be ready at the same time as the "kleftiko". Put a piece of "kleftiko" and some potatoes in every plate. Serve with salad (we suggest "village salad").

Makes 6 dishes.

"ARNI ME FASOLIA" — HARICOT BEANS AND LAMB

1 kilo breast of lamb cut into 2´´ cubes
2 cups of haricot beans
1 cup of onions, coarsely chopped
4 slices of bacon, thinly chopped
2 table spoons tomato purée or 6 tomatoes,
  peeled and chopped
1 celery stick, coarsely chopped
2 tablespoons olive oil
1 cube chicken stock
cooking oil
salt
pepper

Soak the beans overnight. Change the water and put on to boil. Change the water once again and add the onions, celery, bacon, olive oil, tomatoes or tomato purée and stir well. Bring to the boil. Turn the heat down and leave to simmer whilst you fry the meat lightly until light brown. Add the meat to the beans, stir and simmer until cooked.

4 servings.

"ARNI SOUVLA" — SKEWERED LAMB

1½ kilo spring boned lamb
1 cup of dry white wine
1 cup of corn oil
2 stalks of celery, finely
  chopped
2 bayleaves, cut in halves
1 large tomato, finely chopped
½ cup of lemon juice
½ cup of onions, finely chopped
½ tsp of thyme
Salt and pepper to taste.

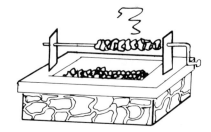

Cut meat in 8—10 pieces. Put it in a big bowl and add all the ingredients mentioned above. Mix well, and leave it there for 2—3 hours to be marinated. Thread them through big skewers, and grill on charcoal for about one hour until they are light brown. The skewers must be turned all the time and very slowly. Every 10 minutes brush meat with the marinate juice left in the bowl. Serve as soon as they are off the skewers, with potatoes that have been cooked unpeeled on the charcoals, or in the oven. Their preparation is very easy; Wash potatoes and while they are wet, sprinkle with lots of salt. Put in a baking tray and put in the oven, for about ½ hour or put them on a grill on the charcoals. Serve meat and potatoes together. Can be accompanied with fresh onions and whole tomatoes and cucumbers.

Makes 6—8 dishes.

"ARNI ME SPANACHI" — LAMB WITH SPINACH —

1½ kilo lamb's neck or shoulder,
    cut in 10—12 pieces
8—10 bunches of spinach
2 tblsps of tomato purée
2 tblsps of lemon juice
1 cup of corn oil
2—3 cups of hot water
2—3 tblsps of yoghourt, for garnish
    in each plate
½ cup of onions, finely chopped
Salt and pepper to taste.

    Clean spinach of its roots and yellow leaves. Put in a bowl of water and add a tblsp salt. Let it stand for 10—15 minutes; (Salt helps to remove the soil). Rinse well and put in clean water. Put oil in a saucepan and fry onions. Then add meat and turn it over until it is light brown on all sides. Add tomato purée dissolved in a cup of hot water. Add 1—2 cups of hot water, more if needed, to cover the meat. Lower heat (to medium) and let cook for about one hour. Put spinach in a sieve and drain. Cut in two pieces. Twenty minutes before the saucepan with the meat is removed from heat put the spinach in it. Add lemon juice and simmer for 20 more minutes until there is a quite thick sauce in the saucepan. Serve hot and accompany with yoghourt and if preferred with a plain rice pilaff.

Makes 8—10 dishes.

81

"CHIRINO" — PORK
"AFELIA" — PORK MARINATED IN WINE

1½ kilo of pork spare ribs
2 tblsps of crushed coriander seeds
1 cup of dry red wine
½ cup of corn oil
Salt and pepper
Hot water as much as needed

Cut the ribs into small pieces, put in a glass pot, ad the wine and the coriander and leave for 5—6 hours to marinate. Then drain the meat. Put the oil in a medium pan to heat and fry the meat lightly. Add wine and coriander and when they come to the boil, add enough water to cover the meat. Add salt and pepper and cook on low heat with the pan covered for about an hour. Serve "afelia" hot accompanied by a pilaff and pour the "afelia" sauce over it. It can also be served with boiled vegetables or even with mashed potatoes.

Makes 6—8 dishes.

Note: In Cyprus potatoes, artichokes and even mushrooms are cooked in the same way as an alternative to the meat.

"CHIRINES BRIZOLES" — GRILLED PORK CUTLETS*

6 pork cutlets
2 cloves of garlic, crushed into paste
1 tblsp of dill, finely chopped
1 tsp of salt
½ cup of green onions, finely chopped
¼ cup of lemon juice
¼ cup of oil
¼ tsp of pepper
¼ tsp of oregano

Take the excess fat off the cutlets. Beat with a meat mallet to flatten them and salt them. Put a grill on the charcoal to get hot and arrange the cutlets on it. Beat oil, lemon juice, garlic, pepper and oregano until they become a thin cream and brush on the cutlets while they are being grilled. Turn over every 10 minutes. Grill for about an hour. Serve hot and sprinkle with dill and onion. Accompany with french fries and a tomato-salad.

Makes 6 dishes.

"CHIRINO ME KOLOKASSI" — PORK WITH CYPRUS TARO

Kolokassi is a kind of vegetable-root, in the shape of a very big sweet potato which is produced in big quantities in Cyprus. Kolokassi preparation is not different from any other vegetable or bulb. The way of cleaning, peeling, and cutting them is explained underneath.

1½ kilo of kolokassi-Taro
1 kilo of boned pork cut in small cubes
1 cup of thickly chopped celery
1 cup of hot water
½ cup of finely chopped onion
½ cup of corn oil
½ cup of tomato purée
½ cup of lemon juice
Salt and pepper to taste
Hot water as much as needed

Scrub kolokassi and dry well with a towel. First cut both ends and peel deep. Hold it tightly with a kitchen towel round it. With a thick blade knife cut slightly and then turn the knife so that a piece of kolokassi breaks. Repeat and chip all round kolokassi. In a heavy deep pan heat oil, put pork cubes to get brown and transfer to a platter. Then pour onions to get soft and add kolokassi to heat for 15 minutes. Cover the pan, hold it and shake well to mix kolokassi with onions and oil. Repeat this 2—3 times, and add pork in the saucepan. Dissolve tomato purée in a cup of hot water and pour into pan. Also add celery and hot water to cover kolokassi. Cover the pan, reduce heat and simmer gently for about 75 minutes until the sauce thickens in the pan. When kolokassi is cooked add salt, pepper and lemon juice.

Serve hot and accompanied with a plate of fresh peeled radishes.

Makes 6—8 dishes

"GOUROUNOPOULO PSITO"
OVEN BAKED SUCKLING PIG

In Cyprus the suckling pig is considered to be a kind of formal food and it has a special place in buffets and parties. In taverns or big restaurants it is served for groups of people by special order. There are very few taverns and restaurants that don't offer this dish. In the country it is barbecued for many people for their relatives from abroad or tourists to whom they want to offer something different from the usual food. We realize that the suckling pig is cooked only when a great number of people are going to eat and this is why it is not included in the ordinary menu of families of 5—6 persons. It is also served on special family occasions such as engagements, weddings, christenings, Christmas, New Year, Easter. It is always cooked whole, barbecued or in the oven and it should not be heavier than 5—6 kilos.

Buy a cleaned suckling pig without intestines. Season its insides first. Put a grill on a big oven-tray and place on it the suckling pig with its abdomen on the grill. Brush corn oil on its outside and put in the oven (medium, 350⁰F) for 2½ hours approximately. Mix in a bowl ½ cup of oil, ½ cup lemon juice, 1 tsp salt, 1 tsp pepper. After an hour, take the pig out of the oven, pour the mixture over it and repeat this every half hour until it is cooked. Use the same method for the barbercued suckling pig, which takes 2 hours to be cooked. Serve hot with baked potatoes and a salad with a variety of vegetables.

Makes 15—20 dishes.

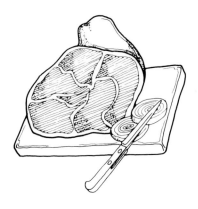

"ROSTO CHIRINO" — ROAST PORK

1½ kilo leg of pork
1 small sprig of rosemary
1 tblsp of corn flour
1 bayleaf
½ cup of thickly chopped onions
½ cup of thickly chopped carrots
½ cup of thickly chopped celery
Salt and pepper

Ask the butcher to remove the skin and half of the fat from the leg. Season and put in an oven-tray. Heat oil in a saucepan and fry the celery, the carrots and the onions. Empty the saucepan's contents in the tray. Put the pork in a hot oven (400°F) to cook for 60—70 minutes. Every half an hour, sprinkle the meat with its own sauce. When it is cooked place the pork in a platter, and put the oven-tray with the remaining sauce on a low heat. Add bayleaf, rosemary, stir with a wooden spoon for about 5 minutes, and until all the contents boil. Add a cup of hot water, stir for 1—2 minutes and pass through a sieve in a pan until completely cold. Then remove all the fat from the surface. Put the pan on very low heat. Dilute corn flour in half a cup of hot water and add it to the sauce. Simmer for 10 minutes and remove from heat. When meat is cold, cut in thin slices and put back into the oven to warm; then pour the prepared sauce over it. Serve the roast pork with mashed potatoes or with a plain rice pilaff or boiled macaroni sprinkled with the same sauce.

Makes 8—10 dishes.

"CHIRINA SOUVLAKIA" — SKEWERED PORK

1 kilo of pork (shoulder)
1 cup of oil
1 large onion whole
1 tsp of cayenne pepper
3 tomatoes cut in slices
3 cucumbers cut in slices
¼ kilo of pork fat
½ cup of lemon juice
½ cup of finely chopped onions
½ cup of finely chopped parsley
Half a lemon for each person
Salt to taste

Cut meat in cubes of about 1 sq. inch. Do the same with pork fat. Put meat and fat in a bowl, add half of the oil, stir and leave for about 1 hour. Peel the whole onion, cut in the shape of a cross so as to obtain 4 pieces and separate every leaf. Then, thread onion leaves and fat in turn on spits so that the meat and the fat are separated by the onion leaves. Place spits on charcoals with low heat and cook until they are brown, for about 1 hour. Add salt to the kebab 15 minutes before they are ready. Mix the rest of the oil with the lemon juice in a bowl and beat well; then brush over the kebab every 10 seconds, every time that the spits are turned on the other side. Serve the kebab hot and garnish each plate with mixed chopped onions, parsley and the cayenne pepper. Add tomatoes and cucumbers cut in slices, as well as half a lemon.

Makes 4—6 dishes.

Note: Kebab is not only served on the plate but also in special "pittes" together with vegetables and various herbs. Please look at page 41 for the recipe of making "pittes".

"VODHINO — MOSCHARISIO"
BEEF AND VEAL

"VODHINO STIFADHO" — BEEF WITH ONIONS*

1 kilo of beef
1½ kilo of very small onions,
   peeled but kept whole
1 cup of oil
4 cloves of garlic, finely chopped
3 bayleaves
10 black pepper corns
2 cups of hot water
1 small piece of cinnamon
½ cup of vinegar
½ kilo of grated tomatoes
Salt to taste

   Cut beef in small cubes. Heat the oil in a casserole, fry the whole onions lightly, take them out of the casserole and put in a platter. Put garlic in casserole until it becomes soft; then fry the beef lightly. Add the vinegar and after it boils, add the tomatoes, salt, pepper, bayleaves, cinnamon and two cups of hot water. Stir, and cook the beef on low heat with covered casserole for about two hours. 30 minutes before removing casserole from the heat, add the onions so that beef and onions are cooked at the same time. Serve hot with vegetables cut in thick slices.

Makes 4—6 dishes.

"SIKOTAKI MOSCHARISIO" — CALF'S LIVER*

1 kilo of calf liver
4—5 peeled tomatoes, cut into cubes
1 onion, finely chopped
3 cloves garlic, crushed
2 tablespoons olive oil
drop of dry white wine
1 cube chicken stock, dissolved
   in ½ cup of water
cooking oil
salt
pepper
cooked rice

   Dice the liver and fry in very hot cooking oil together with onions and garlic. Drain the oil and add the tomatoes, wine, olive oil, stock, salt and pepper and cook on a low heat until the sauce thickens. Serve with rice and make a well which you fill with the liver mixture.

4—6 servings.

87

"VODHINO CASAROLAS" — ROAST BEEF IN CASSEROLE*

1½ kilo of lean beef
1 cup of oil
1 cup of dry red wine
6 cloves of garlic
2 cups of hot water
2 bayleaves
Salt and pepper

Remove fat and membranes from meat. With a small knife, cut small holes in the meat and plant the garlic in them. Heat oil in the casserole and fry the meat on all sides, until it is light brown. Add wine, and after it boils add bayleaves, water, salt and pepper. Let the meat simmer on low heat, with the casserole covered for approximately 2 hours, until soft. Remove casserole from heat, place meat on a tray and when it is almost cold cut in medium slices. Serve with its sauce separately and with various boiled vegetables sprinkled with hot butter, or boiled macaroni covered in meat sauce.

Makes 6—8 dishes.

"VODHINO PAFITIKO" — BEEF A LA PAPHOS

1½ kilo of beef neck
1 kilo of big potatoes
1 cup of corn oil
4 bayleaves
2 tsps of salt
1 tsp of pepper
½ tsp of oregano
½ cup of cold water
½ cup of lamb fat

Cut the beef into 6—8 pieces and place them in a baking tray. Peel potatoes, wash and place them in another tray. Mix salt, pepper and oregano and spread half of them on each tray. Spread also the lamb fat on potatoes, and add half of the oil and two bayleaves. Pour the other half of the oil over the beef and add two bayleaves and ½ cup of cold water, first placing the beef tray in oven on low heat 350°F baking for about 2½ hours until beef is tender. One hour later put the potato tray in oven to bake and to be ready at the same time as beef. Serve hot.

Makes 6—8 dishes.

Note: At Paphos, a province of Cyprus, this kind of food is baked in specially built ovens. After the trays are placed in these ovens, the latter are closed and sealed with a thick mixture of mud. When there is no such oven put the same ingredients in small clay or fire-proof dishes, cover them, and seal them with a paste made of flour and water, and bake in ordinary ovens.

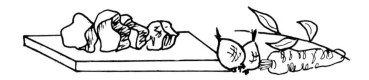

"MOSCHARI ME SALTSA ASPRI" — VEAL WITH WHITE SAUCE

1½ kilos of lean veal
1 cup of sliced onions
1 cup of carrots cut in small cubes
1 cup of potatoes cut in small cubes
1 bayleaf
½ cup of finely chopped parsley

For the sauce:
3 tblsps of butter
3 tblsps of flour
1 cup of hot meat broth
1 cup of fresh milk
3 egg yolks
½ cup of lemon juice

Cut the meat into cubes of about 2 inches. In a saucepan with boiled water put the meat to boil for 5 minutes. Remove the saucepan from the heat and pour away the water. Wash the meat in fresh water. Rinse the saucepan, pour in 8 cups of water, add the meat and heat until boiled. Then add the carrots, onions, bayleaf, salt and pepper. Cover the pan, reduce heat and simmer gently for about 2 hours until meat is tender. Remember to add the potatoes, one hour before removing the saucepan from the heat.

Twenty minutes before the meat is cooked, make the sauce: In a small saucepan heat the butter to melt, add the flour little by little and stir until it becomes a thick white cream. Then add about 2 cups of the simmering veal broth to make the cream thin. Add the milk and simmer for 5 minutes. In a small bowl beat the eggs together with the lemon juice and gradually add one cup of hot broth while stirring.

Empty the egg mixture in the saucepan with the cream, mix together, stir and pour all the mixture back to the saucepan with the meat. Sprinkle over the parsley, stir, heat for another 5 minutes and serve hot, with rice pilaf covered with white sauce.

Makes 6—8 dishes.

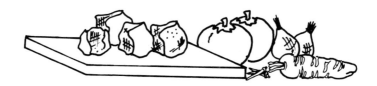

"MOSCHARI ME KHORTA" — VEAL WITH VEGETABLES

1½ kilos of veal shoulder
1 cup of carrots, cut into cubes
    of about ½ inch
1 cup of green beans, finely
    chopped
1½ cup of ripe tomatoes, finely
    chopped
1 tblsp of tomato purée
1 tsp parsley, finely chopped
2 cups hot water
½ kilo of potatoes, cut into cubes
    of about 2 inches
½ cup of chopped onions
½ cup of corn oil
Salt and pepper

Cut the veal into cubes of about 2 inches. Pour the oil into a saucepan to heat and sauté onions, until tender. Add the veal until it is brown and then add water, salt and pepper. Reduce the heat, cover the saucepan and cook the veal for two hours. Then add tomatoes, carrots, green beans, potatoes and parsley and cook for another half hour or until veal is tender. Dissolve the tomato purée in ½ a cup of hot water and pour into the saucepan. Cook for about ½ an hour more, until the sauce thickens. Serve hot with spring onions, tomatoes, and thickly chopped lettuce.

Makes 8—10 dishes.

"MOSCHARI ME PATATES" — VEAL WITH POTATOES*

    1½ kilos of veal shoulder
    1½ kilo of small spring potatoes
    1 cup of white dry wine
    2 cloves of garlic, minced
    1 bayleaf
    1½ cup of corn oil
    2 cups of hot water or meat broth
    ¼ cup of ground onions
    ¼ cup of celery, finely chopped
    ¼ cup of carrots, diced
    ¼ tsp of grated thyme
    Salt and pepper to taste

    Cut the veal into 8—10 pieces, put them in a bowl and add ½ cup of oil, the wine, onions, celery, carrots, thyme and garlic. Mix and leave them for about an hour to marinate. Remove the veal from the marinate and drain it. Pour the oil in a wide saucepan to heat and brown the veal. Add the marinated sauce and vegetables to the veal to boil. Then add water, salt and pepper and the bayleaf. Reduce the heat and cook for about 1½—2 hours. In the meantime peel the potatoes, wash and drain them. Pour 2 cups of corn oil in a frying pan to heat and fry the potatoes until golden brown. Remove them from the frying pan and drain them. Half an hour before the food is ready add the potatoes to the pan in order to absorb the sauce and also to be well cooked. Serve hot.

Makes 6—8 dishes.

91

"VODHINO ROSTO ME SALTSA TOMATA" — BEEF AND TOMATO POT ROAST

1 kilo topside of beef
1 small cup of brandy
4 large tomatoes, peeled
1 beef cube, dissolved in 3 cups of water
1 cup of cooking oil
salt
pepper

Brown the joint on all sides to seal. Remove some of the oil. Chop the tomatoes in quarters and fry them with the beef. Pour over them the brandy and cover. Cook for about 4 minutes. Pour in stock, salt and pepper to taste, cover and cook for about 90 minutes or until beef is tender. Carve beef and pour over remaining sauce. Serve with potatoes of your choice or macaroni.

4—6 servings.

"ROSTO VODHINO" — BEEF POT ROAST*

1 kilo topside of beef
1 glass of dry red wine
1 bayleaf
1 stick cinnamon
3 cloves of garlic
12 pepper corns
4 tablespoons of cooking oil
1 tablespoon of bisto
salt

Slit the beef and insert cloves of garlic. Fry the whole joint on high heat until the beef is coloured on all sides. Add the wine, salt, pepper corns, bayleaf, cinnamon and sufficient water, but do not cover the whole joint. Simmer gently on top of the stove until the beef is cooked. Remove the beef and thicken the sauce with bisto. Cut the beef into slices, pour over the sauce and serve with vegetables and potatoes of your choice.

4—6 servings.

"OSPRIA" — "KHORTA"
PULSE — VEGETABLES

"COLOKASSI MESARITICO" —
COLOCASSI A LA MESAORIAS

The "colocassi" is usually cooked with pork or even with chicken. In Mesaoria part of the Famagusta district they cook the "colocassi" mostly without any meat.

        1½ kilo of colocassi
        3 cups of dry red wine
        1 cup of finely chopped onions
        1 cup of corn oil
        3 stalks of celery
        Salt and pepper

Peel "colocassi" as explained in the recipe "chirino me colocassi" and cut in thick round slices instead of pieces. Place in a pot with wine and leave for about 2 hours. Then drain. Put oil in a casserole; when it is hot fry onions with celery. Add "colocassi" and stir from time to time for 5 minutes. Add wine and after it boils well add 2 cups of boiled water. Then add salt and pepper, lower heat and cover the casserole. Simmer for about two hours, until the sauce becomes thick.

Makes 6—8 dishes.

93

"IMAM BAYILDI" —
EGGPLANTS WITH TOMATO SAUCE*

This is a Turkish dish but it is cooked by all the inhabitants of the island because of its nice smell and taste.

      1 kilo of medium size eggplants
      1 cup of oil
      1 kilo of grated ripe tomatoes
      1 cup of onions cut in round slices
      1 cup of hot water
      1 cup of finely chopped parsley
      ½ clove of garlic in every eggplant
      Salt to taste.

Remove the little stalks from the eggplants. Cut each one in two lengthwise and remove half of its skin. Sprinkle with salt and leave for approximately 20 minutes so that all their bitter water comes out. Then wash eggplants well, drain and plant the piece of garlic in every piece. Fry in hot oil on both sides till they become brown. Place them in a casserole in rows. Fry the onions in the saucepan and add parsley and tomatoes. Add the salt, stir and let the sauce simmer for about 20 minutes. Pour the sauce in the casserole over the eggplants add a cup of hot water, and simmer for half an hour or till the sauce becomes thicker. Serve "Imam Bayildi" hot as a "meze" or as garnish with fish or meat.

Makes 6—8 dishes.

"FASOLIA SOLIATICA" — HARICOT BEANS A LA SOLEAS

    1 kilo of haricot beans
    3 small stalks of celery, finely
       chopped
    1 cup of ripe tomatoes, finely
       chopped
    1 tblsp of tomato purée
    ½ cup of corn oil or olive oil
    ½ cup of onions, finely chopped
    ½ cup of smoked bacon cut into
      small pieces
Salt and pepper to taste

Rinse the dry beans the night before cooking them, and put them in cold water for about 10 hours. The following day put them in a saucepan with clean water to boil for about 10 minutes. Remove from the heat and leave them to cool. Change the water, cover the pan, reduce the heat and cook for about ½ an hour. In the meantime pour the oil in a frying pan to heat and sauté onions and celery. Then, add the bacon, the tomatoes and the tomato purée dissolved in a cup of water. Stir, and cook on low heat for about ½ an hour. Then empty the mixture into the saucepan where the dry beans are. Five minutes before the food is ready add salt and pepper. Serve hot with black olives and onions.

    At Solea, a Cyprus district, as well as in the whole island of Cyprus dry beans are served as a main dish especially during lunch time. They can also be served as a side dish with meat or fish.

Makes 8—10 dishes.

"DHIAFORA KHORTA STO FOURNO" — VARIOUS OVEN BAKED VEGETABLES*

1 cup of grated cheese
1 cup of ripe grated tomatoes
1 tblsp of tomato purée
1 cup of hot water
2 green peppers cut in thin rings
5 cloves of garlic, finely chopped
6 fillet of anchovies
¼ kilo potatoes cut in long
  thick slices
¼ kilo eggplants cut in long
  thick slices
¼ kilo zucchini cut in long
  thick slices
½ cup of olive oil
½ cup of corn oil
½ cup of finely chopped parsley
½ cup of finely chopped celery
½ cup of pitted black olives
  finely chopped
½ tblsp of oregano
½ cup of finely chopped onions
Salt and pepper to taste

Butter a baking-tray and place in rows the potatoes, zucchini and eggplants. Spread half of the cheese. Spread over cheese the green pepper, celery, oregano and anchovies. In a frying pan heat the two kinds of oil and put garlic to get golden. Add onions, olives and stir until soft. Dissolve tomato purée in a cup of hot water and pour in the pan. Add parsley, grated tomatoes, salt and pepper. Simmer the sauce for 15 minutes and pour over the vegetables. Spread over the remaining cheese and place the tray in low heat oven for about 50 minutes. Serve mixed vegetables hot or cold as garnish or as a nice "mezé".

Makes 10—12 dishes.

"ANGINARES ME AVGOLEMONO"
ARTICHOKES WITH EGG AND LEMON SAUCE

8 globe artichokes
1 tblsp of lemon juice
1 tblsp of olive oil
2 tblsps of chopped parsley

For the sauce:
1 tblsp of corn flour
2 cups of chicken broth
2 tblsps of lemon juice
3 egg yolks
Salt and pepper

To prepare the artichokes:
Cold water
The juice of one lemon
2 tblsps of flour
2 tblsps of salt

First prepare artichokes: In a bowl of cold water pour the juice of lemon, the flour and the salt. Place each artichoke in the water, remove it and cut off the stalk. Pull off all the hard outer leaves. With a knife cut off the inside leaves until only the heart remains and drop it in the prepared water. In a saucepan of boiling water pour the olive oil, salt and lemon juice and then pour artichokes to boil for about 40 minutes until tender. Drain artichokes and place them on a platter. Now prepare the sauce: Bring chicken broth to boil. In a cup dissolve corn flour with a little of cold water and pour in the broth little by little while stirring. Let boil for two minutes and remove from the heat. In a bowl beat the egg yolks with the lemon juice and add gradually a half cup of hot chicken broth beating at the same time. Pour egg mixture to the broth, add salt and pepper and stir. Heat the sauce for two more minutes and pour lemon sauce over artichokes. Sprinkle them with parsley and serve hot.

Note:
This "avgolemono" sauce can also be used for boiled fish and meat or any other boiled vegetables.

"BAMIES YIAHNI" — OKRA WITH TOMATO SAUCE*

1 kilo of okra
1 cup of oil
1 cup of ripe tomatoes, peeled and
    finely cut
1 tblsp of tomato purée
3 cloves of garlic, finely chopped
1 bayleaf
½ cup of vinegar
½ cup of chopped onions
½ cup of parsley, finely chopped
Hot water (as much as required)
Salt and pepper to taste.

Wash the okra and drain them. Cut off their stalks (be careful not to cut the okra because if cut they will melt during cooking) put them in a platter, sprinkle them with vinegar and salt and place them under the sun to wither. Pour the oil into a frying pan to heat and sauté the okra. Empty the okra in a saucepan. Then sauté the onions and garlic and add the tomatoes. Dissolve the tomato purée in a cup of hot water and pour it into the frying pan. Stir and cook for about 15 minutes. Then empty this sauce into the saucepan with the okra and add enough hot water to cover them. Reduce the heat, cover the saucepan and cook for about 40 minutes, until the water evaporates. When ready, sprinkle them with parsley and serve hot. This food is served as a main dish especially during the religious fasting days. It is also delicious with roast beef or fish.

Makes 4—6 dishes.

"KOLOKITHAKIA YIEMISTA ME RIZI"
STUFFED ZUCCHINI WITH RICE

10 medium size zucchini
2 cups of hot water
1 cup of rice
1 cup of ripe tomatoes, finely chopped
½ cup of corn oil
½ cup of olive oil
½ cup of tomato purée
½ cup of finely chopped parsley
½ cup of finely chopped onion
½ tsp of dry mint
½ cup of grated cheese
Salt and pepper

Cut ends of zucchini and wash. Cut a thin slice lengthwise from each zucchini. With a teaspoon scoop out most of zucchini flesh leaving a thick wall, and shaping them like boaks. Heat the corn oil in a frying pan and fry zucchini to get golden from all sides. Transfer them on a platter. Then put in the pan the onions until soft and add the rice. Stir for a while and add parsley, chopped tomatoes, salt, pepper and one cup of hot water. Stir and cover the pan. Reduce the heat and simmer the mixture until all water is absorbed. Remove pan from heat and when half cool blend in the mixture the grated cheese and the mint. With this mixture fill the zucchini and place them in rows. Dissolve tomato purée in a cup of hot water and pour over zucchini. Pour also the half cup of olive oil. Cover the saucepan and simmer the stuffed zucchini on low heat for about 45 minutes until a thick sauce remains.

Makes 6—10 dishes.

99

"GLYKISMATA" — PASTRY

"VASILOPITA" — SANTA CLAUS CAKE

Vasilopita is a cake containing a coin following a Cypriot custom. It is made especially for New Year's day, and it is cut a few hours after the end of the past year, when the people are still sitting around the tables eating and enjoying themselves on the New Year's Eve. The "vasilopitta" is cut into pieces and distributed to the members of the family or to the relatives who happen to be present and the one who finds the hidden coin is considered to be the lucky one of the year.

5 cups of flour
2 cups of butter
2 cups of sugar
1 cup of fresh lukewarm milk
2 tblsps of yeast
1 tblsp of aniseed
9 eggs
1 cup of blanched split
  almonds
½ cup of sesame seeds
½ tsp of salt

In a small saucepan boil aniseed with one cup of water and pour through a strainer into a bowl. In another bowl dissolve yeast in warm milk and add one cup of flour. Stir until it thickens. Cover with a thick serviette and leave it for about an hour to rise. Heat butter slightly to melt. Beat 8 eggs with sugar. Mix the salt in the rest of the flour and make a hollow in the middle. Pour into the hollow the yeast dough made an hour before, the aniseed juice and mix well. Add butter and beaten eggs and knead for about 20 minutes until cream like. Cover again with a thick serviette and leave for about an hour to rise. Knead again for 5 minutes and pour into a greased pastry dish. With a new blade cut different shapes on the surface of the dough. Spread the surface with 1 beaten egg, and sprinkle with sesame seeds and almonds. Place the dish in a moderate oven so that the cake bakes slowly for about 70—80 minutes. After baking let it cool and remove from the dish. With a knife make a deep slit on the side of the cake and insert a coin (wrapped in a small piece of foil) in the slit.

"FLAOUNES" — EASTER CHEESE CAKES

During the Easter feast days in every Greek Orthodox house you happen to visit either in towns or in small villages, you will come across "flaounes". A purely Cypriot celebratory speciality which is traditionally prepared with great piety and care by Cypriot housewives. It is not just prepared because of religious tradition but also because it is delicacy for everyone. In fact most of the housewives prepare a greater number of "flaounes" than needed, in order to be able to serve them not only on Easter feast days but also several weeks or even months later. Their preservation is achieved using the known method of drying. Two or three days after the Easter holiday all the left over "flaounes" are re-heated and can be preserved for a long time. Nowadays the "flaouna" is so popular that it is not only baked for traditional religious purposes but it can be found at any time of the year at confectioneries, teaparties, cocktail-parties etc. The main ingredient used for preparing the "flaouna" is a special kind of cheese made by the shepherds of the island. Also the Cypriot hard cheese known by the name "kefalotyri" or even "halloumi". In case it is difficult to find one of the above mentioned kinds of cheese, use a kind of hard cheese like the English Cheddar or Cheshire, the Italian Parmesano or Pecorino or even the French Cautal Cheese.

Here it is the recipe of the famous Cyprus "Flaouna" which is highly recommend to you.

For the dough:

1 tsp of resin pounded and mixed with 1 tsp of sugar
5 cups of flour
1 cup of warm water
1 cup of melted butter
1 tsp of yeast
3 eggs
½ cup of warm milk
½ tsp of salt

For the stuffing:

1 kilo of hard cheese, grated
10 eggs
2 tblsps of dry mint
1 cup of sultana raisins
2 tsps of baking powder
1—2 beaten eggs
½ cup of sesame seeds

Preparation of the stuffing:

Mix cheese with raisins and mint. Add eggs and mix to thicken. Cover with a woolen cloth and leave for 2—3 hours. A quarter of an hour before using add baking powder.

Preparation for the dough:

Mix flour, salt, resin and yeast dissolved in water. Add butter and knead. Add the eggs one by one, milk, water and knead until dough thickens and does not stick on your hands. Cover with a woolen cloth and leave for about an hour. Roll up the dough to a thickness of ⅛ of an inch. Cut into circles with a diameter of about 6 inches. Place in the centre of each circle 2 tblsps of the stuffing and fold the sides to form a square shape. Using a fork press the four sides of the square to join. Brush the beaten egg over the "flaounes", sprinkle with sesame seeds, put them in a greased pan and bake in a moderate oven of 350⁰—400⁰F for 35—40 minutes until golden brown.   Makes 25-30 pieces

"DHAKTYLA" — STUFFED SMALL PASTRY
(LADIES FINGERS)

For the dough:

3 cups of flour
1 cup of water
1 tsp of salt
2 egg yolks
½ cup of corn oil or butter

For the stuffing:

1 cup of pounded almonds
2 tblsps of sugar
¼ cup of pounded walnuts
½ tsp of cinnamon powder
The whites of two eggs

For the syrup:

1 cup of sugar
3 cups of water
1 small cinnamon stick
2 cloves
1 tblsp of lemon juice
½ cup of honey

For garnish:

½ cup of chopped almonds

Pound the almonds and put them in a bowl. Add the rest of the ingredients for the stuffing and mix well until thick. Then pour salt and oil to flour, mix well and add egg yolks, water little by little and knead until dough thickens. Cover it with a thick serviette and leave for about half an hour.

In the meantime prepare the syrup. Place all the ingredients in a saucepan and heat slowly for 10 minutes until it thickens slightly. Roll out the dough into a thin layer and cut it into rectangular pieces (11X9 cm). In the centre of each piece, place 1 teaspoon of the stuffing. Fold over each rectangular piece and with the help of a fork press the two ends to join. Fry "dhaktyla" in plenty of corn oil and drain in a strainer. Before they cool soak in syrup and strain again. Place them in a platter and sprinkle with chopped almonds.

Makes about 40 pieces

"LOKMADHES" — CYPRUS DOUGHNUTS WITH HONEY SYRUP

"Lokmades" are small, round fried balls of dough dipped in syrup. However simple the actual making of the lokmadhes is, much patience is needed in preparing the mixture, skill in cutting the dough, and quickness in frying and dipping the lokmadhes into syrup. That is why there are only a few housewives who make them. However we come across "lokmades", at fairs in the mountains, by the sea or in villages, where there are people who specialize in making and selling them the year round, because for the Cypriots, "lokmadhes" are a delicacy. In towns or large villages there are small shops which sell only "lokmadhes". However, let us see how these delicious, aromatic little balls are made.

For the dough:

2 cups of flour
1 table spoon of yeast
2 cups of warm water
1 tea spoon of salt

For the syrup:

1 cup of sugar
1 cup of water
1 small stick of cinnamon
½ cup of honey
½ cup of rose water
1 table spoon of sugar
mixed with cinnamon

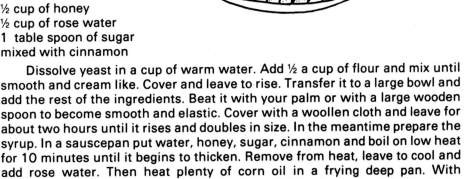

Dissolve yeast in a cup of warm water. Add ½ a cup of flour and mix until smooth and cream like. Cover and leave to rise. Transfer it to a large bowl and add the rest of the ingredients. Beat it with your palm or with a large wooden spoon to become smooth and elastic. Cover with a woollen cloth and leave for about two hours until it rises and doubles in size. In the meantime prepare the syrup. In a sauscepan put water, honey, sugar, cinnamon and boil on low heat for 10 minutes until it begins to thicken. Remove from heat, leave to cool and add rose water. Then heat plenty of corn oil in a frying deep pan. With your left palm take some of the dough, then slightly close your palm so that a small ball comes out. Cut it with a teaspoon and put it to fry in the hot oil. Fry 20-25 lokmadhes each time. While frying separate them by using a big spoon. Fry until golden brown. Put in a strainer and while hot dip into cold syrup. Put them on a platter and sprinkle with a mixture of cinnamon and sugar.

Note: The above recipe is to my opinion a very original one in Cyprus. There are, however, some people who add potato purée to the mixture to make them more crunchy. The proportion is 2 cups of flour and 1 cup of potato purée.

"PISHIES" — PASTRIES WITH SYRUP

For the dough:
3 cups of flour
1 cup of corn oil or butter
1 cup of water
1 tsp of salt
3 eggs
1 tsp of cinnamon powder

For the syrup:
1 cup of sugar
2 cups of water
3 cloves
1 tblsp of lemon juice
½ cup of honey
½ cup of rose water

Mix flour with salt, and half of the oil and mix. Add eggs, and water little by little and knead until dough thickens. Cover with a serviette and leave for about an hour. In the meantime prepare the syrup.

Pour all the ingredients into the saucepan and place on low heat for about 10 minutes until it starts to thicken, and remove from the heat. Knead dough for a while and cut into four balls. Roll out each ball into thin circles, brush them with oil and sprinkle with cinnamon. Shape each circle for second time into a ball and roll out into thin circles. Brush them with a bit of oil and sprinkle with cinnamon. Finally, roll up each circle into a long roll and cut off small round pieces, about one inch thick. Roll out the pieces lightly to become small flat cakes and fry them in a lot of boiling oil until golden. Remove from the frying pan, put into a strainer then dip into syrup while still hot and strain again. Sprinkle with sugar powder and serve hot.

Note: In the old times, in Cyprus, "pishies" were made with the same ingredients but instead of being fried, they were cooked in specially made pans which were placed on lit coals and honey mixed with water was used instead of syrup.

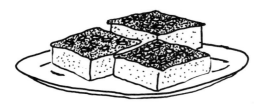

"SHIAMALI" — SEMOLINA CAKES

For cake mixture:

2 cups of semolina
1 cup of sugar
1 cup of yoghurt
½ cup of corn oil
½ tsp of baking powder
½ tsp of vanilla powder
½ cup of rose water
¼ cup of blanched chopped almonds

For the syrup:

1 cup of sugar
1 cup of water
1 tsp of lemon juice

Put the semolina in a bowl and mix with oil. Add all the ingredients except almonds and mix well. Pour the mixture into a greased tray, sprinkle with almonds and place the tray in the oven on medium heat to bake for about an hour until golden brown. Remove tray from the oven to cool. In the meantime boil on low heat, the water, sugar and lemon juice for about 10 minutes. While the cake is still warm cut into small triangular or rectangular pieces and cover with syrup.

"RIZOGALO" — RICE PUDDING

4 cups of fresh milk
1 cup of rice
1½ cup of sugar
1 tblsp of corn flour
2 egg yolks
2 cups of water
1 tblsp of cinnamon powder
½ tsp of vanilla powder

Wash rice well in a strainer and put in a small saucepan. Add water and boil for about 10 minutes. Add milk. When it starts to boil, add sugar. Dissolve corn flour in two tablespoons of water and beat together with egg yolks and vanilla. Pour the egg mixture slowly into the saucepan and stir using a wooden spoon. Simmer for 2—3 minutes, remove from heat and pour it into small bowls or into a big bowl. Sprinkle with cinnamon, leave to cool and put in the refrigerator.

"GLIKO TOU KOUTALIOU"
FRUIT PRESERVES IN SYRUP

The "gliko tou koutaliou" is prepared from fruit or even from small vegetables like eggplants, carrots, or almonds, which are cooked in syrup. In Cyprus the "gliko tou koutaliou" is to be found in every home. It is the first thing to be offered to every guest to a Cypriot home. Whether a relative, friend, tourist or stranger, all are bound to be offered the "gliko" served with a glass of water as soon as they enter the house.

The Cypriot housewife who is so much praised for her hospitality prepares the "gliko tou koutaliou" with great care and mastery, following the old tradition.

Most Cypriot housewives were taught by their mothers when they were still young girls how to prepare the "gliko", which they later offer with great pride.

Cyprus, their country, where every kind of fruit is plentiful, gives them the opportunity to make the "gliko" all the year round.

The island produces so much fruit, like cherries, apples, pears, watermelon, green walnuts, grapes, quinces, dates, oranges, grapefruit, bitter oranges and others, that the housewife can choose to prepare a variety of "gliko" which she can offer at any time to her visitors.

From such a great choice of "gliko", we in our turn selected a variety of "gliko" recipes which we believe will be to your liking.

"GLIKO KERASI" — CHERRIES IN SYRUP

1 kilo of cherries, ripe but hard
1 kilo of sugar
1½ cup of water
2 tblsps of lemon juice
½ tblsp of vanilla powder

Wash cherries, strain, remove stalks and remove pips with the help of a cherry bobber.

Put water and sugar in a saucepan and heat until sugar melts. Add cherries and increase heat. Boil the "gliko" for 30 minutes until syrup thickens.

In the meantime remove foam 3—5 times. 5 minutes before removing the pan from the heat add lemon juice and vanilla.

Leave to cool and transfer to clean, sterilized, dry jars with lids.

Keep in cool place where there is no sun.

Note: In order to ensure that the syrup is as thick as it ought to be dip a tsp into the syrup and place it above a glass full of water so that the syrup drips into the water. If the syrup dissolves before reaching the bottom of the glass, it requires more thickening. If it arrives at the bottom and does not dissolve, it is ready.

"GLIKO KITROMILO" — BITTER ORANGES IN SYRUP

20 bitter oranges
1½ kilo of sugar
3 cups of cold water
2 tblsps of lemon juice
½ tsp of vanilla powder

Slightly grate bitter oranges to remove the red colour which covers their skins. In each bitter orange make a slit in the shape of a cross so that you get 4 pieces of skin. Remove the fibres from the inside of the skins, roll the skins and tie with a white thread so that they remain rolled while cooking. Then place in glassbowl of cold water and leave for 3—4 days. Change the water daily. On the fourth day place them in boiling water and heat for about 20 minutes until they soften. Remove from boiling water and place on a thick serviette so that it absorbs their water. In a small, sauce pan pour the water, add sugar stir and after 5 minutes add the rolled skins to boil on high heat for about 40 minutes until syrup thickens. 5 minutes before removing the sauce pan from the heat add vanilla and lemon juice. Leave the "gliko" to cool and transfer into sterilized, dry jars with lids. Keep in cool place.

Note: In the same way you can prepare "gliko" from orange skins.

107

"GLIKO MILO" — APPLES IN SYRUP

1 kilo of small unripe apples
1 kilo of sugar
1½ cup of water
2 tblsps of lemon juice
4 lemons
½ tsp of vanilla powder

Using a special apple corer remove cores of apples taking care not to remove the stems. With a knife peel the apples. Place them one by one in cold water containing the juice of 2 lemons. Pour some water in a saucepan to boil. Then add apples and heat for about 15 minutes until they soften. In the meantime pour some cold water in another saucepan, add the juice of the last two lemons and dip the softened apples to cool. Take them out of the saucepan and place on a kitchen towel so that it absorbs their water. Pour water into a saucepan, add sugar, stir, heat for about 5 minutes and add the apples. Increase the heat to the full and boil apples until syrup thickens. In the meantime remove foam 3—4 times. 5 minutes before removing the saucepan from the heat add 2 tablespoons of lemon juice and the vanilla. When the saucepan is removed from the heat leave until the following day and then heat again on maximum heat for about 15 minutes until the water evaporates. Leave them to cool and place in sterilized, dry jars with tight lids. In so doing the "gliko" may be preserved for 9—12 months.

Note: With the same amount of ingredients small half-ripe pears can also be made into "gliko".

"GLIKO MELINTZANAKIA" — SMALL EGGPLANT IN SYRUP

1 kilo of small tender eggplants,
   of about 2 inches long
1 kilo of sugar
2 cups of cold water
2 tblsps of fresh lemon juice
2 vanilla sticks
5 cloves
Almonds

Blanche the same number of almonds as of eggplants. Remove coves from eggplants, and with a knife partly remove skins making the shape of a cross. Make a slit in the side of each eggplant and place them one by one in plenty of cold water. Leave for about 24 hours changing the water 3—4 times during this period. Cover eggplants with a plate or a saucepan lid so that they are submerged in water. The next day put them in a strainer to drain. In each slit of the eggplant put an almond and tie some thread around the eggplant so that the almond does not fall out during cooking. Lay them out on a cloth to dry. In a saucepan put sugar, water, cloves, vanilla, heat to boil and add eggplants. Boil for about 6 minutes. Remove saucepan from heat and leave for 24 hours. The following day put eggplants in a strainer and remove threads from eggplants. Place saucepan with syrup on very high heat to boil, add eggplants and heat until syrup thickens. Every 5 minutes remove foam with a sieve. 5 minutes before removing saucepan from fire add lemon juice. Allow eggplants to cool and put in jars.

"TA ESPERIDHOEDI STIN KYPRO" —
THE CITRUS FRUIT IN CYPRUS

Cypriot citrus fruit are famous for their quality, taste and aroma, and there is a great demand for them on the international market.

The climate of Cyprus and most of its soil are ideal for growing these trees. In addition, the Government's great interest, support and scientific help, which it offers to the cultivators of citrus fruit, lead to the continual increase of the production of citrus fruit in Cyprus and a significant improvement in their quality.

Today finest quality oranges of various kinds are being produced in Cyprus (like Valencia, Oval, Navel), as well as lemons, grapefruit, tangerines, clementines and others.

As the production of citrus fruit increases, so does the amount exported to various countries, such as the Arab countries, the European Economic Community, East and West Europe, the Scandinavian countries and others. For the period beginning September 1977 to June 1978 the exports of citrus fruit amounted to 10.175 tons. Apart from the exports, a substantial amount of citrus fruit are consumed by the Cyprus people and by the tourists.

The Cypriot housewife does not omit to add citrus fruit to her diet and additionally to prepare various sweets and drinks from them.

The following recipes are made by Cypriot housewives who have not been influenced by machinery and science and who continue to prepare them in the traditional way using no preservatives, colours or any other artificial substances.

Unreservedly, I present to you some of the recipes, and I believe that you will greatly enjoy them.

"PORTOKALADHA SIROPI" — ORANGE SQUASH

4 cups of orange juice
3 cups of sugar
1 cup of cold water
3 leaves of fresh basil
½ cup of grated orange peel
½ cup of lemon juice

Wash oranges, dry and grate some to get the grated peel needed. Squeeze oranges in a glass bowl, add grated peel to orange juice and leave for about half an hour until juice is aromatic. Then pour the juice through a thin cloth or a fine strainer so as to remove the grated peel.

Transfer juice into a saucepan, add sugar and basil leaves and place on medium heat. Stir slightly for a while and when sugar is dissolved increase heat to boil. Add lemon juice and remove saucepan from heat. Leave to half cool, remove basil leaves and transfer syrup into well washed and sterilized bottles.

When completely cool close the bottles with sterilized corks and keep the bottles in a cool place away from the sun or in the refrigerator if there is room.

Orange squash is a nice refreshing drink served throughout the year and especially in the Summer.

Way of serving: In a high ball glass pour 2 oz squash, add 3—4 ice cubes, a slice of fresh orange, fill glass with water or club soda or tonic water, stir well and serve.

Makes about 44 oz.

111

"MANTARINADHA" — TANGERINE SQUASH

4 cups of tangerine juice
3 cups of sugar
2 cups of water
3 cloves
¼ cup of lemon juice
The peel of two tangerines

Peel tangerines and squeeze them. Put sugar, water and cloves in a saucepan and heat until a running syrup is formed. Then add tangerine juice and tangerine peel and increase heat to boil. Remove saucepan from heat and add the lemon juice. Leave to half cool and transfer into sterilized bottles. Keep them in the refrigerator.

It is served in the same way as orange squash

Makes about 45 oz.

"LEMONADHA SIROPI" — LEMON SQUASH

4 cups of lemon juice
4 cups of sugar
4 cups of cold water
½ cup of grated lemon peel
The peel of a lemon

Wash lemons, dry and grate some on a fine grater to get the necessary grated peel.

Squeeze lemons, add grated peel to lemon juice and leave for about half an hour. In the meantime pour the water and sugar in a saucepan and heat until syrup is runny. Pour lemon juice through a fine strainer. Add lemon and lemon peel to syrup. Increase heat and when starting to boil, remove from fire. Leave to cool, transfer into well washed and sterilized bottles and seal them with new sterilized corks. Place the bottles in the refrigerator.

If there is no room for them in the refrigerator, keep them in a cool and dark place.

Way of serving: In a big high glass pour 2—3 oz. squash. Add 3—4 ice cubes, a slice of fresh lemon, fill the glass with water, soda water or tonic water, stir and serve.

Makes about 50 oz.

"ANAMIKTO SIROPI" — MIXED FRUIT SQUASH

2 cups of orange juice
2 cups of bitter orange juice
1 cup of tangerine juice
3 cups of sugar
2 cups of cold water
3 leaves of fresh basil
2 cloves
½ a cup of lemon juice

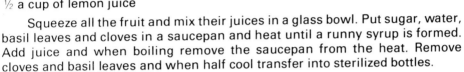

Squeeze all the fruit and mix their juices in a glass bowl. Put sugar, water, basil leaves and cloves in a saucepan and heat until a runny syrup is formed. Add juice and when boiling remove the saucepan from the heat. Remove cloves and basil leaves and when half cool transfer into sterilized bottles.

It is served in the same way as all the other squashes.

Makes about 45 oz.

"LIKER MANTARINI" — TANGERINE LIQUEUR

4 cups of pure alcohol
4 cups of sugar
6 cups of cold water
4 cloves
1 tsp of lemon juice
The peel of six tangerines

Wash the six tangerines, dry and peel them. Clean the peel well, so that no white substance remains on the inside part and grind it twice using a vegetable or meat grinder. Pour in bottles with screwing lids and add alcohol. Close the bottles and expose them to the sun for about 10 days.

On the eleventh day put the water, sugar and cloves in a saucepan and heat slowly until a runny syrup is formed. Remove saucepan from heat and when half cool add lemon juice. Remove cloves and pour it into the bottles with the alcohol. Close the bottles and place them again in the sun for 10 more days.

Then, pour the liqueur through some cotton or special paper filters and transfer into ordinary, sterilized bottles with screwing lids.

Keep liqueur in a cool place away from the sun.

Makes about 90 oz.

"LIKER PORTOKALIOU" — ORANGE LIQUEUR

5 cups of sugar
8 cups of cold water
3 cups of pure alcohol
1 cup of V.S.O.P. brandy
6 cloves
2 cinnamon sticks
1 tsp lemon juice
The peel of three oranges

Peel the oranges carefully so that there is no white substance left on the peel. Wash the orange peel, dry and grind it twice using a meat grinder. Put it in bottles with screwing lids. Add to the peel the appropriate proportions of brandy and alcohol in each bottle, close the bottles and expose them to the sun for 10 days.

On the eleventh day, put the water, sugar, cloves and cinnamon sticks in a saucepan and heat until a runny syrup is formed. Remove syrup from heat. Remove cloves and cinnamon sticks from syrup, add the lemon and when cool pour into bottles.

Close the bottles and place them again in the sun for 10 more days. Then, pour the liqueur through special paper filters into ordinary sterilized bottles with screwing lids.

Place orange liqueur in a cool place away from the sun.

Makes about 120 oz.

"LIGA LOGIA" — A FEW WORDS

I have referred in a pedantic manner to most of the recipes of Cypriot dishes and beverages. I did this in an attempt to present to you, the way of preparing these Cypriot dishes and also to inform you as much as possible on the history and customs of Cyprus, and the way of presenting Cypriot food and drink, thus giving you a picture of Cypriot life and its character.

Talking about Cypriot food and beverages it would be an omission not to mention Cyprus wines and alcoholic drinks which are closely connected to them.

I therefore take this opportunity to give some information on this subject.

115

"TA KRASIA TIS KYPROU"
THE WINES OF CYPRUS

HISTORY

Cyprus was one of the first countries to cultivate vineyards and to develop wine distilleries. This is primarily due to its geographical position near the Mesopotamia border known to be the first country to plant vineyards. More evidence is given by archaeological findings like the amphora now seen in the Cyprus museum and dated to 900 B.C., the famous Paphos mosaics representing the God Dionysus (or Bachus) with the inscription (ΟΙ ΠΡΩΤΟΙ ΟΙΝΟΝ ΠΙΟΝΤΕC) — the first who drank wine — the historian Hesiod who lived in 735 B.C. and who described the manufacturing of the sweet wine "NAMA". The arrival of King Richard the Lionheart to Cyprus in 1191, and, in the same year, the Lusignians who renamed "NAMA" to the well known "Commandaria" which is still being manufactured in exactly the same way today as it was then. It is said that the Turkish occupation of Cyprus in 1571 is due to the fact that the then Sultan Selim II tasted Cyprus "Commandaria" offered to him by a wine dealer and ordered the seizure of Cyprus.

THOSE WHO ADMIRE IT

Before ending the history of Cyprus wine, I would like to mention a few of the many people who have praised it:

Hesiod, Greek Poet, Circa 800 B.C.

"When I rise, I want either to massacre or to quench my thirst drinking Cyprus wine."

Elisabeth Browing

"Cyprus wine is as sweet as the lyres of the Muses. It has the colour of the lion and shines brighter than ever did the eyes of the Paphos Goddess; it is as light as her step."

Ludolf Von Sudheim, 1340 A.D.

"In the diocese of Paphos lies the vineyard of Engadi, which has not its equal in the whole world".

Richard The Lionheart

"I must return to Cyprus if only to taste its wine again."

Mark Antony To Cleopatra As He Gave Her The Island

"Your sweetness, my love, is equal to that of Cyprus Nama."

Sultan Selim II, 1571

"We must capture Cyprus. In this island there is a treasure which only the King of Kings is worthy of possessing."

Bishop Arnuf Of Lisieux Circa 1200 A.D.

"Cyprus wine is sweet, but stuns if not mixed with water."

Reverend Papaconstantinos From Ayia Anna Village Of Larnaca

"Óssi mínes mé tó "Ró" tó krasí chorís neró,
Óssi mínes dhíchos "Ro" tó krasí mé tó neró."

In all the months that include the letter "R", do not mix the wine with water. In the months that do not include "R", mix the wine with water.

I learned this saying from Reverend Papaconstantinos, who was taught it by his great grandfather.

WINE FESTIVAL

Nowadays as in the past, Cyprus wine is honoured at a special celebration known as "The Wine Festival". Every year around the middle of September special festivities lasting a fortnight are being organised in the Limassol Municipal Garden. The organising of "The Wine Festival" is undertaken by the local Town Hall in co-operation with the big wine firms who are willing to offer free wine to the festival visitors. The festival includes Cyprus dancing competitions between Cypriot and foreign dancing groups, songs, plays and other festivities. Restaurants are set up serving mostly Cypriot food. There are a lot of kiosques selling souvenirs, ceramics, bottled drinks and miniatures. There is also a Government Post Office selling special envelopes with Cyprus stamps. Foreigners from all over the world meet at the "Cyprus Wine Festival" and together with the well known hospitable Cyprus public enjoy themselves in a brotherly atmosphere until morning hours.

TODAYS QUANTITIES

The sun shines over Cyprus for more than 330 days each year and the winter snow and rain provide enough water for irrigation during the long hot summer — ideal conditions for the cultivation of the vine. The southwest of the island is dominated by the Troodos range of mountains rising to the peak of Mount Olympus, 6,400 feet high. It is mainly on the lower slopes of these mountains that the vines are grown.

118

TODAYS QUANTITIES

This ideal place where the vine yards are to be found, the suitable climate for them and the great interest on the part of the Government have contributed to creating that world known fame, attributed to the Cyprus wines whose exports are increasing incessantly.

The United Kingdom imports about 5 million gallons of Cyprus wine including sherry of various types. Cyprus, in fact, is the third largest supplier of wines to the British market, following France and Spain. Already, Cyprus wines appear on tables in France, Italy and Germany, all major wine producing countries themselves. Other importing countries include Sweden, Denmark, Canada and some 25 others. Today the wine industry is in a position to supply the U.S.A. not only with quality wines but also in quantity. The wine industry now ranks as the second largest in Cyprus, bringing $12 million in foreign currency and making the island the world's highest per capital wine exporter.

THE QUALITIES

In Cyprus every owner of a small or a big vineyard produces wine for his own use, and sells the rest of his grapes to the wine distilleries which undertake wine making and export. The biggest wine distilleries in Cyprus, are four: KEO, SODAP, ETKO-Hadjipavlou and LOEL. The products of these four wine distilleries are of exceptional quality and many of them have won gold and silver medals at international exhibitions. The goods they produce are of a great variety and can be served with all kinds of dishes: for example, the famous "ouzo" with its excellent aroma of aniseed; the sherries which are well known abroad; the vermouths; all sorts of wines, liqueurs; vintage brandies; champagnes; and others. In our island, there is also a great consumption of beer which is produced by the KEO and CARLSBERG breweries. Newly developed drinks are also popular, such as Cyprus V.O. brandy, which is served at evening receptions of various types. The V.O. brandy is also used for the making of the popular and well known long drink "brandy sour" which is greatly liked and praised by people visiting this island.

119

THE QUALITIES

The following quotation is from one of the so many admirers of brandy sour. He wrote it to me after I served him his first brandy sour.

I have known Nick a short time but he has that bubbling infectuous personality which makes you feel like you have been friends for a lifetime. Nick is one of our loyal and faithful barman at the Canadian Contingent Officers Mess in CYPRUS. He has the solution – liquid or verbal – for almost any mood and problem. His liquid solutions are of the exquiste variety + well balanced with just the right mixture. My favourites are his Brandy Sour and Martini. But Nick's real value to us Canadians is his easy fun loving character. He is truly a fine representative of the Cypriot people

R S Billings
Commanding Officer
8th Canadian Hussars

I have known Nick a short time but he has that bubbling infectuous personality which makes you feel like you have been friends for a lifetime. Nick is one of our loyal and faithful barman at the Canadian Contingent Officers' Mess in Cyprus. He has the solution — liquid or Verbal — for almost any mood and problem. His liquid solutions are of the exquisite variety — well balanced with just the right mixture. My favourites are his Brandy Sour and Martini, but Nicks' real value to us Canadians is his easy Fun loving Character. He is truly a fine representative of the Cypriot People.

In my opinion all these good words were said not because I have the "magic touch", to what we usually attribute a good drink but rather to the excellent quality of Cyprus products which I think were worth introducing to you.

THE QUALITIES

THE CYPRUS BRANDY SOUR

The Cyprus brandy-sour is the most famous drink on the island and is also very much liked by tourists and other visitors to Cyprus. The secret of its success is the perfect combination of Cyprus Brandy and Cyprus lemon squash. I am afraid to say, that if it is not prepared in Cyprus and especially without Cyprus products, we are likely to prepare a drink which will not be the real Cyprus brandy-sour.

The reason for this as I have mentioned above, is due to the perfect combination of Cyprus Brandy and Cyprus lemon squash. Its preparation is very simple and I shall give it to you with pleasure.

For a bottle carrying 40 fl oz use the following ingredients:

22 fl oz of brandy V.O.
16 fl oz of lemon squash and
¾ of 1 fl oz of Angostura bitters.

Pour all the ingredients in a bottle, shake the bottle well for a while and put in the refrigerator. Before we go on to the final preparation I would like to stress that in Cyprus this drink is served as a long drink and not as a cocktail with a mixture of egg white and other ingredients as it is served in other countries.

In a glass with a capacity of 10 fl oz pour 2 oz., of the bottle mixture. Add two dashes of Angostura to make its aroma stronger, add 3—4 ice cubes, and fill the glass with club soda. Add a slice of lemon or, according to preference, a slice of orange. Stir well and serve.

A small sprig of fresh mint can also be placed on top of the drink.

EPILOGUE

    I feel very happy because I have been able, through my book, to communicate with you and thus accomplish a duty which, as I have already mentioned in my introduction, I was so much concerned about. I have chosen for you some very original Cypriot food recipes and I have tried to present them to you as simply as possible. It does not mean however that, with the recipes which appeared in my book, the Cyprus cuisine chapter is closed because this in fact never ends. I have written for you the most traditional recipes and I hope that once you have tried them out you will have additional delicious dishes.in your daily diet. After you have tried them a few times and you have achieved the right taste, your family and your friends will be grateful to you.

    Good luck and bon appetit

    Thank You,

Nearchos Nicolaou
(NICOLAS)
The author

INDEX